Ky

An Essay on Government

The Library of Liberal Arts
OSKAR PIEST, FOUNDER

AN ESSAY ON
GOVERNMENT

By
JAMES MILL

Edited with an Introduction by
CURRIN V. SHIELDS

Chairman, Department of Government,
University of Arizona

A LIBERAL ARTS PRESS BOOK

THE BOBBS-MERRILL COMPANY, INC.
INDIANAPOLIS • NEW YORK

THE LIBERAL ARTS PRESS
A Division of
THE BOBBS MERRILL COMPANY, INC.
Printed in the United States of America
ISBN 0-672-60215-6 (pbk)
Sixth Printing

CONTENTS

AN ESSAY ON GOVERNMENT

5

THE POLITICAL THOUGHT OF
THE BRITISH UTILITARIANS

James Mill occupies an important place in the history of modern political thought as the chief disciple of Jeremy Bentham, founder of the British Utilitarian movement.

Of the thinkers who influenced nineteenth-century British life, perhaps none was the equal of this brilliant legalist and dedicated philanthropist. An eccentric, versatile, dynamic thinker, and a prolific author, Jeremy Bentham (1748-1832) attracted a coterie of followers, the Benthamites. The group included Francis Place, "the Radical tailor of Charing Cross" who devised techniques of partisan political action; David Ricardo, the high priest of classical political economy, the counting-house wing of Utilitarian liberalism; James Mill's eldest son, John Stuart, the middle-class philosopher of common sense; and John Austin, the champion of analytical jurisprudence. It included as well Alexander Bain, Henry Sidgwick, George Grote, Lord Henry Brougham, Sir Francis Burdett, Joseph Hume, Sir Samuel Romilly, and many other lesser figures who in their own way left an imprint on British life. They sat at the feet of the master and were nourished by his creative genius. They founded the *Westminster Review* (in 1824) to propagate Benthamite opinions, and University College, London (in 1828), to spread his teachings.

It was these inspired Benthamites who built that remarkable ideological edifice, Utilitarianism, the creed so many nineteenth-century British intellectuals accepted along with Newton's laws of motion. For the Benthamites went out into the world as teachers, lawyers, writers, civil servants, politicians, and other men of public affairs to preach—and practice —the Utilitarian gospel. The Utilitarians, and especially the younger Benthamites called the "philosophical radicals," did make their influence felt in many areas of British thought and practice: education, local government, public health, civil administration, penology, civil law, foreign trade, colonial policy, all came within the Benthamite orbit.

I

Bentham was primarily a legal theorist with a proclivity for reform. His first published work (at the age of twenty-eight), *A Fragment on Government* (1776), was an attack on a theory of law expounded in Sir William Blackstone's *Commentaries on the Laws of England*. His best-known work was *An Introduction to the Principles of Morals and Legislation* (1789). Though the younger Mill's remark that Bentham "found the philosophy of Law a chaos, he left it a science" claims more than the facts warrant, it is true that Bentham's avowed lifetime ambition was to discover "the true principles of the legal science."

For Bentham legal science is a means to a practical end: reform of the system. The prevailing legal system favors special privileges for the few at the expense of the happiness of the many. By changing the laws, the evils embalmed in the system can be eliminated. What is needed, therefore, is a set of workable principles—"scientific" principles—to guide legal reform. For such reform, normative principles are of course imperative. The true science of legislation must include both the study of what the law is and what the law ought to be. The science of what the law is Bentham called "expositional jurisprudence." Where expositional jurisprudence stops, "censorial jurisprudence" begins. The difference is that censorial jurisprudence provides an objective standard for evaluating the law as it is. After all, the subject-matter of both studies is the same: human nature. Expositional jurisprudence, then, tells us what the law is now; censorial jurisprudence tells us what it ought to be, to conform to "the nature of man." Thus for Bentham legal reform consists in adapting the laws of the state to the principles of human nature which "experience" reveals.

Every program for political change is founded on some theory of "human nature" which includes both psychological and ethical conceptions. Bentham's theory was not original with him: David Hume, Helvetius, Joseph Priestley, and other eighteenth-century "moral philosophers" had advanced similar conceptions. But it was substantially in the form fashioned by Bentham that this theory of human nature became part of the intellectual baggage of many nineteenth-century British thinkers, and certainly of all those Utilitarians who wrote impressive treatises on law, political economy, government, and society.

In the opening passage of the *Principles of Morals,* Bentham declares: "Nature has placed mankind under the governance of two sovereign masters, *pain* and *pleasure.* It is for them alone to point out what we ought to do, as well as to determine what we shall do. On the one hand the standard of right and wrong, on the other the chain of causes and effects, are fastened to their throne." Pain is what nature prescribes for man; pleasure is what nature commands that man seek. Individuals naturally seek to avoid pain and obtain pleasure, or, more exactly, to obtain an excess of the amount of pleasure over the amount of pain. For though all pleasure is of the same kind, the amount of pleasure an individual can obtain does vary. An act may, for example, yield pleasure of more or less intensity, or duration. What gives an individual the most pleasure, he alone knows. Since an excess of pleasure over pain is "happiness," each individual is the best judge of his own happiness. According to this theory of human nature, then, it is the psychological nature of man to seek happiness. We can explain human actions only by the pursuit of individual self-interest in happiness.

For Bentham this theory is a prescription of how men should behave, as well as a description of how they do behave. His formulation of the theory is rather crude, but apparently what links his hedonic psychology to his utilitarian ethics is the concept of "reason," a familiar concept in the thought of eighteenth-century *philosophes.*

The "first principle of morals," the universal and exclusive principle, the *sole* guide in determining how men ought to act, is, Bentham declares, *the principle of utility*—"that principle which approves or disapproves of any action whatsoever, according to the tendency it appears to have to augment or diminish the happiness of the party in question." This principle all men do invoke, more or less, to guide their actions. But individuals *should* always be guided by the principle of utility. The moral choice confronting an individual, then, is that he can act to achieve more happiness, or less.

In these Benthamite terms, a moral judgment is necessarily a rational judgment. The pursuit of pleasure non-rationally is self-defeating. To achieve the *greatest possible* amount of happiness an individual must act rationally. Fortunately, men are, by nature, rational animals. What distinguishes rational action is (a) a conception of a desired end and (b) an understanding of the best means to attain it. The rational individual first calculates the desirability of an end, then he calculates how he could best achieve the end through action. Not the character of an act, nor the intent of the individual, but rather the actual consequences determine the moral validity of an act. Since the amount of happiness it yields in practice is the measure of the utility of an act, rational calculation of its probable effects is required to judge an act's morality. When an individual in the pursuit of his self-interest acts according to the principle of utility, he acts to achieve the desired end of happiness by the desirable means of "reason."

So though "nature" tells us what we shall do—seek happiness—"reason" tells us what we ought to do to conform to our nature. We ought to pursue our individual self-interest rationally. We ought to use the principle of utility to guide all our actions, in order to achieve the greatest happiness. The Benthamite ethics may be described as a theory of how men should act to obtain, through rational means, what they naturally desire—the greatest possible amount of happiness.

II

In his theory of legislation Bentham attempted to project this principle of utility, propounded as a guide for individual action, to the social level. The Benthamite guide for collective action by a group of individuals is the principle of *social* utility. It was at this point—the relation between the greatest happiness of the individual and the greatest happiness of the greatest number—that the Benthamites encountered some perplexing theoretical difficulties.

In studying society, Bentham contends, we must start with the basic datum of an existing society. A political society exists when a number of individuals (subjects) are supposed to be in the habit of paying obedience to other individuals in authority (governors). In any particular society this habit of obedience is neither perfectly present nor absent; obedience is always a matter of more or less. But the habit of obedience, in quantitative terms, indicates the vigor and strength of a society. The more acts of obedience predominate over acts of disobedience, the more that society displays the attributes of an organized political society.

Consequently, what distinguishes an organized political society is the presence of constituted offices, "institutional machinery" for making and enforcing laws. Laws consist in rules for guiding the actions of rational individuals. The essence of law is the command of a political superior to inferiors over whom authority is recognized. Law has therefore two qualities: it must be expressed and enforced. The political superiors who make and enforce laws in a society are "sovereign." On sovereign authority there is no legal limit; as the source of law, the sovereign cannot be subject to it. But a constitution does define in law how a sovereign shall exercise authority.

Obedience by subjects does not necessarily indicate approval of the law, or even of the authority behind it. But why then do individuals obey, or disobey, laws? Law, says Bentham, implies a duty to obey or be punished. By law pain is inflicted, in the form of punishment for violation; by implication, pleasure is granted as the reward for obedience. Subjects obey a law so long as the disadvantages of obedience are less than the disadvantages of disobedience. If it is to his interest, for an individual, to obey the law and avoid punishment, he does so. If not, he refuses. But it is to the *best* interest of the subjects that laws be enforced; everyone recognizes, as by a kind of tacit agreement, that to some extent all individuals have a common stake in the maintenance of peace and order. Likewise it is to the *best* interest of the governors that commands be obeyed. A command that is not enforced is not in fact law; it lacks authority. Thus the curb on the sovereign's authority is disobedience by the subjects.

Bentham's contention is that obedience to authority depends in practice on the rational pursuit of self-interest. Subjects obey the law so long as the governors exercise authority in accord with the subjects' interests, so long as the law yields more pleasure than pain for them. Hence in practice the fundamental test of law is "utility"—the amount of happiness a law yields for individuals subject to the governors' authority.

For Bentham it is this theory of law, a description of law in practice, which occupies the realm of expositional jurisprudence, that study instrumental to the inquiry into what the law ought to be. Knowledge of *how* to promote the greatest happiness by granting rewards and imposing punishments through legislation is the realm of censorial jurisprudence.

Bentham's formulation of the principle of social utility is that in legislating "the sole measure of right and wrong is the greatest happiness of the greatest number." How can the greatest happiness be determined? Since "society" is merely a fiction to express the notion of a collectivity of individuals, social utility must of course be computed in terms of individual happiness. The proper procedure is to calculate a law's consequences for individuals; it is a matter of adding and subtracting sums of individual happiness. How much would the law increase the happiness of some, and decrease the happiness of others? A law's social utility is thus measured by its contribution to the greatest happiness of the greatest number. Since a law ought to promote the greatest happiness, the guide in legislating ought to be the principle of social utility.

Jeremy Bentham was a legalist, not a politician. In fact he became interested in political reform at all only late in life, under the influence of James Mill. Earlier Bentham had confidently assumed that men act rationally to promote their self-interest in happiness. Hence if you explain to a man the rational way for him to act in promoting his interests, he will act accordingly. So far as men do pursue their self-interest rationally, the greatest happiness of the greatest number necessarily results. Rulers, rational men too, will legislate according to the true principles of legal science—if only they are told.

Relying on this belief, throughout much of his lifetime Bentham diligently appealed to political leaders to adopt the reforms he proposed. He lobbied with some of the most influential rulers of his time, in different countries. A few, such as Lord Shelburne, were among Bentham's close acquaintances. He attempted for years to persuade British rulers, for example, to adopt his proposal for penal reform, the "Panopticon"; it was in 1791 that he first approached Pitt with the scheme. But these attempts were without avail. The experience of a lifetime of telling taught Bentham that something was amiss. First to his surprise and then to his disappointment, Bentham found his wise counsel ignored by those he was so eagerly trying to help. By 1802 he had become thoroughly disillusioned about politics and disgusted with politicians. How to explain this "unnatural" behavior? Why do rulers fail to promote the greatest happiness of their subjects, after they are told how to do so? What can be done about it?

James Mill tried to answer these questions for the Benthamites. It was Mill who converted Bentham, by birth and habit a Tory, to radicalism. It was Mill who attempted to explain why British statesmen and jurists apparently do not desire the greatest happiness of the British people. And it was Mill who offered a program for doing something about it. It was as a result of Mill's efforts that Bentham's Utilitarianism was ultimately transformed from a theory of legal reform to a creed of political action.

III

James Mill was born April 6, 1773, in a Scottish village, the son of the shoemaker. He attended the parish schools and a nearby academy, and thanks to the generosity of a wealthy patron, he was sent in 1790 to the University of Edinburgh to study theology. He distinguished himself as a Greek scholar; while still continuing his studies he served as a tutor. In 1798 Mill was licensed as a preacher by the Scottish Church. But he found this calling not to his liking; in 1802 he abandoned Scotland and the ministry for a literary career. He accompanied his patron, who had been elected a member of Parliament, to London. A few years later, in June, 1805, Mill married a Harriet Burrow; his first-born child was named after his Scottish benefactor, Sir John Stuart. Eight more children followed in Malthusian order. For years the Mill family was plagued by financial difficulties. Mill did manage to eke out a bare existence for his family through his journalistic efforts, but more than once Mill was dependent on the generosity of affluent friends such as Francis Place, whom Mill met in 1812.

About the same time that his famous son was born, in 1806, James Mill started work on the book which eventually established his literary reputation and shaped his career, *The History of British India*. After twelve years of strenuous labor, the three-volume book, the first work of its kind, was completed and finally published in 1817. It was an immediate success. In 1819 Mill received a post with the East India Company; later, in 1830, he was made head of the India Office.

It was in 1808 that James Mill met, through the good offices of a mutual friend, the man whose disciple he was to become. Jeremy Bentham and Mill soon became close friends. The Mills lived for years in a house owned by Bentham; they frequented his Devonshire country place, Ford Abbey, for extended periods of residence. For a quarter of a century, until Bentham's death in 1832, Mill and the founder of Utilitarianism were intellectual companions and collaborators.

What was the relation between these two unusual men? The French historian, Halévy, remarks that "Bentham gave Mill a doctrine, and Mill gave Bentham a school." [1] Mill's contribution was considerable; his influence on Utilitarianism was profound. In Halévy's words, Mill served as "the indispensable intermediary between Bentham and the external world." [2] Bentham was something of a recluse, living apart from the world of affairs. It was around Mill that the Benthamites actually gathered; despite his austere, pedantic character, it was from him they took their lead. Mill was the dominant figure in the Benthamite circle.

Mill performed another, an exceedingly important, function. Prior to Mill's influence on Bentham, the distinctive Utilitarian ideas had been diverse in origins, somewhat disconnected, and rather crudely formulated. Bentham had borrowed them from where he found them, to provide a rationale for the legal reforms he desired. Mill, a rigorous and systematic thinker, integrated these ideas into an elaborate Utilitarian philosophy embracing, in addition to a theory of jurisprudence, theories of education, political economy, and government as well. And he also provided a doctrinal foundation, in his "associationist" psychology, for Bentham's pleasure-pain principle and his principle of utility.

Then of course James Mill was by profession a publicist. He devoted his literary talents to the Benthamite cause, as "the enthusiastic propagandist." This was no minor service.

[1] Élie Halévy, *The Growth of Philosophical Radicalism* (1949 ed.), p. 251.

[2] *Ibid.*, p. 308.

Bentham's writings were devoid of literary elegance; they were discursive and repetitious; they were suffused with words of his own coinage. To be understood, Bentham's writings required at least an editor; through a translator his ideas could be best comprehended. It was mainly by James Mill's writings, in fact, that the Utilitarian tenets reached the public.

Mill's literary career began as a contributor to the *Anti-Jacobin Review*, edited by his friend, John Gifford; Mill's articles began to appear in 1802. The next year he became, through Gifford's sponsorship, the editor of the *Literary Journal*, an ill-fated publication which lasted from 1803 to 1806; during that period Mill also edited for the same publisher the *St. James Chronicle*. In 1804, Mill wrote a pamphlet entitled "An Essay on the Impolitic Nature of a Bounty on the Export of Corn." In 1805, a translation by Mill of C. F. Villers, *Spirit and Influence of the Reformation of Luther,* was published. Another free-trade pamphlet by Mill, "Commerce Defended," appeared in 1808. That same year Mill became a frequent contributor to the influential Whig journal, the *Edinburgh Review;* his first article on "Money and Exchange" was followed by essays on the constitutions of Spanish-American republics, China, and the East India Company. Between 1802 and his death on June 23, 1836, James Mill contributed dozens of articles on a variety of subjects to numerous journals—in addition to those already mentioned, the *British Review, Eclectic Review, Quarterly Review, Philanthropist, Annual Review, Westminster Review,* and the *London Review.*

Though a prolific author of essays, today Mill is no doubt better remembered for his few books than for his many articles. In addition to *The History of British India,* Mill wrote two well-known books: *Elements of Political Economy,* and *Analysis of the Phenomena of the Human Mind.* The *Elements* (1821) was designed as an introductory textbook; in fact the book was based on tutorial instructions in political economy Mill had given his son, John Stuart. In this treatise Mill expounds, simply and directly, the classical economic doctrines espoused by his intimate friend, David Ricardo. Like Ricardo, Mill accepts those economic implications of the Malthusian theory of population that led Carlyle to brand the study "the dismal science." Mill's *Elements* became a popular handbook for British liberals who advocated a policy of laissez-faire.

In the *Analysis* (1829) James Mill attempted to "make the human mind as plain as the road from Charing Cross to St. Paul's." His aim was to construct a foundation in psychology for Benthamite principles. Following David Hartley, Mill tries to explain "mental phenomena" by the principle of "association of ideas." This two-volume work was Mill's most ambitious, if not most influential, philosophical enterprise.

In all these writings, James Mill, the faithful Benthamite, propagated the gospel of Utilitarianism. In fact in his last published treatise not long before his death, *A Fragment on Mackintosh* (1835), Mill launched a spirited counter-attack in answer to certain criticisms of Utilitarianism advanced by Sir James Mackintosh in *Dissertation on the Progress of Ethical Philosophy* (1830).

Most significant as expositions of Utilitarianism, however, is a series of essays Mill wrote between 1816 and 1823 for the Supplement to the Fifth Edition of the *Encyclopaedia Britannica*. He contributed articles on "Jurisprudence," "Liberty of the Press," "Education," "Economist," "Benefit Societies," "Colony," "Prison Discipline," "Beggar"—and most importantly, an essay on "Government."

IV

James Mill's essay on "Government" is, as Ernest Barker has said, "the classical statement of the political theory of the Benthamites." [3] Though its general thesis was anticipated in

[3] The essay was written in 1819 and published in 1820. It was reprinted during the 1820's in several editions, including one private edition for gratis distribution, in which the authorship was not acknowledged but with the symbols "F.F." used to identify Mill's Supplement articles. In

an earlier article Mill wrote for the *Edinburgh Review* (January, 1809), and its ideas are found dispersed in other of his writings, the essay on "Government" (which, according to John Stuart, the Philosophical Radicals regarded as "a masterpiece of political wisdom") is without doubt the most succinct, as well as the definitive, formulation of Utilitarian political theory.

In the essay Mill addresses himself to a quite utilitarian task: to determine the proper relation between the individual and authority. Of course this relation must be explained in terms of "interest," the rational self-interest of individuals in happiness. A theory of government, Mill postulates, must adequately answer two central questions: What is the proper end of government? What is the best means for attaining it? In answer to the first question Mill reformulates as a political doctrine Bentham's greatest happiness principle. In answer to the second, he propounds his doctrine of representative government.

What is the proper end of government, dictated by "human nature"? To be sure, it is the greatest happiness of the greatest number of individual citizens. But why? The government's authority, Mill argues, depends on the self-interest of individuals. What is that interest? "To increase the utmost pleasures and diminish the utmost pains." This is happiness. How does an individual achieve happiness? The natural basis of pleasure, says Mill, is satisfaction in obtaining "objects of desire." Pain is lack of such satisfaction. How are desires satisfied? By means of the products of labor, the material goods and services produced through human ingenuity and industry. Since the demand for objects of desire far exceeds the supply of goods and services, everyone cannot satisfy to the full their desires.

Under these circumstances, how can the greatest possible happiness be achieved? The greatest happiness of the greatest

1828, a collection of these articles, including the essay on "Government," was published, with Mill's authorship recognized. Apparently it was this edition which gave the essay its wide reading audience.

number, computed by adding up amounts of individual happiness, is possible when each individual rationally pursues his self-interest, when each does the best he can for himself. "Greatest possible happiness in society is attained by insuring each man the greatest possible quantity of the produce of his own labor." Happiness increases as individuals are allowed to acquire as much wealth as their industry and talent make possible.

What, then, is the end of government? Government is founded on the fact of human nature, "that one human being will desire to render the person and property of another subservient to his pleasure, notwithstanding the pain or loss of pleasure which it may occasion to that other individual." To avoid such violations, government is formed; government exists "when the greater number of men combine and delegate to a smaller number the power necessary for protecting them all." Government, it follows, is merely a means, an agent charged by the members of society with protecting the property of individuals from violation by others.

To achieve its end, government should interfere with individuals as little as possible: the less government, the better. Government means restraint on individuals, necessary restraint on a few to protect the many. Even so, the fewer restraints, the greater the liberty of individuals, hence the greater happiness. In short, government promotes the greatest happiness of the greatest number negatively, as a dutiful policeman, by securing for each individual the opportunity to pursue his self-interest unmolested.

What is the best means for achieving this end? What is the best system of government for promoting the greatest happiness of the greatest number of individuals? The human appetite for happiness, Mill argues, is insatiable; there is no limit on the amount individuals desire. Nor is there any limit on the political means to the end of happiness—power, the ability to inflict pain and grant pleasure. Yet if government is to perform its function effectively, power must be vested in public officials. The difficulty is that public officials, like other individuals, seek to satisfy their self-interest at the expense of others; they tend to abuse the power entrusted to them. Hence a dilemma: satisfaction of individual interests requires that authority be vested in public officials, yet power in the hands of public officials offers a serious threat to the greatest happiness.

How can the abuse of political authority be prevented? Mill initially discusses this question in the traditional terms of the three "pure" forms of government—by one, the few, and the many. Monarchy and aristocracy he dismisses as undesirable; the interests of the rulers conflict with the interests of the greater number of ruled. He likewise dismisses, on the same grounds, a "mixed" form of government incorporating all three principles. With democracy the interests of the ruler and the ruled do coincide, since the people literally rule themselves. But though democracy may be desirable in theory, it has a great drawback in practice: the business of government—legislating, administering, and adjudicating public policies—cannot be conducted democratically. Indeed, democracy is a practical impossibility.

Mill's solution is of course representative government. Unless individuals can express and enforce their interests politically, those interests are at best ignored and at worst violated by public officials. The interests of citizens can be adequately expressed and enforced by representatives, provided the interests of the representatives coincide with those of the citizens. The representatives in assembly can exert control over public officials; through their legislative representatives, citizens can prevent the abuse of authority by executive and judicial officials.

But a problem still remains. How can the interests of the community be kept in harmony with the interests of the representatives? How can the abuse of authority by representatives be prevented? This can be done, Mill holds, by making the representatives politically responsible to the citizens. The representative can be elected for a short term of office by the vote of a majority of citizens residing in a constituency. The majority's vote for a representative can reflect the sum of the greatest number of individual interests in a constituency. The elected representative's interests coincide with those of his constituents: either he promotes their interests in the assembly or he is turned out of office at the next election. By this system, the citizen can check on his representative, who in turn can check on the government officials. The result: good government. Mill concludes that a system of representative government, properly constituted, does make possible the greatest happiness of the greatest number of individuals.

V

Mill's essay is both a definitive statement of Utilitarian political theory and a most vivid exhibition of the method of inquiry employed by the Benthamites. The Benthamites believed that a true science of government is possible and can be developed if only "experience" is properly investigated. The task is to extend the method of reasoning used in the physical sciences to the "moral sciences."

What is the method of science? Scientific reasoning is like mathematical reasoning. First you formulate a universal law which nature reveals to be true. From this axiomatic truth you deduce, as Newton did, scientific principles. Reason, then, yields knowledge of the principles which govern nature and these principles provide criteria for ultimate truth. Not just logical or empirical truth, but moral truth as well. So Mill declares that "the whole science of human nature must be explored to lay the foundation for a science of government." By this method of reasoning it is possible to infer from "a few simple principles of human nature" a scientific theory of government. Such a theory Mill endeavors to propound. After his declaration that the end of government is the greatest happiness of the greatest number, the remainder of his essay on "Government" is a series of logical arguments by which political principles are deduced from "human nature."

This essay led Thomas Macaulay, then a rising young Whig

intellectual, to characterize Mill as "an Aristotelian of the fifteenth century, born out of due season." In a review article for the *Edinburgh Review,* Macaulay subjected the Benthamite method as exhibited by Mill to a scathing criticism.

We have here [writes Macaulay] an elaborate treatise on Government, from which, but for two or three passing allusions, it would not appear that the author was aware that any governments actually existed among men. Certain propensities of Human Nature are assumed; and from these the whole science of Politics is synthetically deduced! [4]

This *a priori* method, he charges, is altogether unfit for an investigation of political principles. "Our objection to the Essay of Mr. Mill is fundamental. We believe that it is utterly impossible to deduce the science of government from the principles of human nature." [5] Certainly a science of government is possible, as the Benthamites believe, but that requires, as Francis Bacon well knew, an inductive method of reasoning.

After his father's death, John Stuart Mill, the legitimate heir to the Benthamite tradition, confessed that Macaulay's charge was well-founded. The Utilitarians had taken geometry as their model, as had Hobbes and Newton. This was a mistake, for it led them to base their arguments on insufficient empirical data. The *proper* method, said the younger Mill, is the "Concrete Deductive Method: that of which astronomy furnishes the most perfect . . . example." [6] There, as in the moral sciences, laboratory experiments are impracticable. But the astronomer can analyze complex events and discover the underlying primary laws, and he can test the calculated combined effects of those laws by further observation. This is the scientific method the political scientist ought to employ. It was this model of astronomy that Stuart Mill had in mind

---

[4] *Edinburgh Review,* Vol. 49 (March, 1829), p. 161. This article touched off a debate with the Benthamite journal, the *Westminster Review,* which continued for several issues in both journals.

[5] *Ibid.,* p. 185.

[6] J. S. Mill, *A System of Logic* (8th ed., 1874), p. 619.

when he wrote, as a loyal Benthamite: "The backward state of the Moral Sciences can only be remedied by applying to them the methods of Physical Science." [7] By mid-century the "moral scientists," led by the later Utilitarians, virtually dominated British political thought, as well as economic, legal, and social thinking. The aim of a science of politics was accepted; the only question was how to apply the "scientific method" in political inquiry.

Of course this view was not shared by all, and the claims of the "political scientists" did not go unchallenged. In the course of the debate the issue was clearly drawn. Is it enough for political thinkers to act and think "like scientists"? Is the method of inquiry used so successfully in the physical sciences at all suited to the study of politics? This notion of a science of politics entertained by his lifelong friend, the younger Mill, Thomas Carlyle summarily rejected. He charged that it was the preoccupation of British thinkers with logic and science that led them into "the barren wastes of materialism," blinding them to the realities of life. The underlying difficulty is that the scientific method cannot be used to investigate that invisible world of the human "spirit" which makes men—as the German philosophers well know—what they are:

In the field of human investigation, there are objects of two sorts: First, the *visible,* including not only such as are material, and may be seen by the bodily eye; but all such, likewise, as may be represented in a *shape* before the mind's eye, or in any way pictured there: And secondly, the *invisible,* or such as are not only unseen by human eyes, but as cannot be seen by any eye; not objects of sense at all; not capable, in short, of being *pictured* or imagined in the mind or in any way represented by a *shape* either without the mind or within it. [8]

When the attempt is made to study mankind scientifically, much that is most significant and distinctive about political societies is missed.

[7] *Ibid.,* p. xiv (from the synopsis of the Table of Contents).

[8] T. Carlyle, "The State of German Literature," *Edinburgh Review,* Vol. 46 (Oct., 1827), p. 339.

The burden of Carlyle's charge is that the scientific method is not suited to the study of human subject-matter. Politics, like all studies devoted to "human investigation," is not and can never become "scientific." This charge points up the crucial issue at stake in the controversy over method of political inquiry, as the problem was formulated by the Benthamites. Is the subject-matter of politics sufficiently different from that of the physical sciences as to make the scientific method inapplicable in political inquiry? After all, the Benthamite conception of method of inquiry depended on an assumed analogy: that political phenomena are like physical phenomena. If the analogy holds, then the problem is to get political thinkers to employ the methods of inquiry used so successfully by the physical scientists; what counts is the attitude and skill of the investigator. But if the analogy does not hold, there is no ground for believing, as the Benthamites did, that a science of politics is possible.

With the publication of Charles Darwin's *The Origin of Species* in 1859, and the intellectual revolution which followed in the wake of the theory of organic evolution by natural selection, the character of the controversy over method of political inquiry changed radically. Darwinian theory shook the foundations of nineteenth-century thought. Biology became the queen science. During the past century the course of intellectual development has in large measure been marked by efforts to trace out in other realms of inquiry the implications of Darwinian conceptions. Devotees of "political science" naturally sought the key to method in biological conceptions; the historical-comparative method in its many variations displaced the older analytical conceptions.

As a result of Darwin's influence, the methodological principles confidently embraced by the Benthamites and exhibited by James Mill in the essay on "Government" have become hopelessly outmoded. Now the question of whether a science of government, such as contemplated by the Benthamites, is possible is, to put it mildly, far from settled. What is settled is that even if the purpose of political inquiry is to discover scientific principles of politics, the Benthamite method, viewed from a perspective of more than a century of intellectual development, is a grossly inadequate means for achieving that purpose.

VI

Utilitarianism is of course no exception to the generalization that every political theory rests on certain assumptions about human behavior. Indeed, James Mill deliberately based the Benthamite doctrines on a "science of man." Yet a theory is no sounder than the assumptions on which it rests. Just as the Darwinian influence served to undermine the rationalistic foundations of the Benthamite method of inquiry, so did Darwinian conceptions show that the rational pursuit of self-interest in happiness is a much too simple explanation of political behavior. Present-day schools of psychology do not entirely agree on a theory of human behavior. Even so, they do concur that the Benthamite theory of "human nature," with its assumptions about the relation between thought and action, rests on an unsound empirical foundation. Like the Benthamite methodological principles, the *a priori* psychological principles invoked by Mill have proved in the course of time to be something less than realistic.

Perhaps the most incisive critical analysis of the Benthamite theory of human nature was advanced, significantly, by the political theorist mainly responsible for introducing the modern psychological approach to the study of politics, Graham Wallas. Wallas' first book to embody post-Darwinian psychological conceptions, *Human Nature in Politics* (1908), was in part devoted to an attack on what he termed "the intellectualist fallacy." He contended that nineteenth-century thinkers, following the Benthamites, assumed *a priori* "a few simple principles of human nature" which grossly oversimplified the psychological facts. The rational aspects of human thought and action were exclusively stressed, while the nonrational were completely ignored. The result was a conception of human behavior in politics which "tended to exaggerate the intellectuality of mankind."

Wallas charges that the Benthamites make three assumptions about human behavior which experience fails to support: (1) that all action results from thought; (2) that all thought is rational; and (3) that all thought results in action.

The Benthamites assumed that a human action is a necessary result of a conscious intellectual process: first a man thinks of an end he desires, then he calculates the best means for attaining it. But, Wallas urges, this assumption actually accounts for only some actions. In the first place, men sometimes act without thinking at all. A man may act from impulse, without consideration of the end or means of action; for example, men do not choose "to run away in battle, to fall in love, or to talk about the weather in order to satisfy their desire for a preconceived end." Secondly, even when thought does precede action, that thought may be non-rational rather than rational. Rational thought is an artificially acquired skill; it depends on observance of certain man-made rules of logical inference; it requires conscious effort to direct the thought-processes purposively; it takes place only at a level of full consciousness. But experience indicates that men draw "natural" as well as logical inferences; that they think in the absence of willed purpose; that thought-processes go on in the subconscious. Such non-rational thought may well serve as the basis for human action. Finally, Wallas points out, experience shows that not all thought results in action. Though we may "think out" a line of action, it does not follow that we will be motivated to act accordingly. We may not act at all, or we may act "irrationally."

We are forced to conclude, Wallas argues, (1) that not all action is based on thought; (2) that not all thought is rational; and (3) that not all thought results in action. The abstract, formalistic assumptions of the Benthamites are simply contrary to the facts of human psychology. The "rational political man," contemplated by thinkers like Mill, is, like its economic counterpart, at best a misleading fiction.

In the course of elaborating his criticism of Benthamite intellectualism, Wallas advanced a conception of human behavior, again mainly based on the findings of the then new science of psychology as he comprehended them. Central in Wallas' conception, which has throughout a strong Darwinian flavor, were the assumptions (1) that thought and action result from the interrelation between human nature and the environment, and (2) that important facts about human behavior concern the role played by "instincts." We must remember, Wallas holds, that man has an animal nature. Instincts—more or less constant "impulses towards definite acts or series of acts independent of their probable effects"—are natural to man in the sense that they are biologically-inherited attributes of the species, primitive carry-overs into civilized times from earlier stages of evolution. An instinct is a cause of action when properly stimulated; the potency of an instinct depends on the stage it appeared in the evolution of the human organism, the older being the stronger instincts. Instincts are many and varied, and at least some are in direct conflict. Men "naturally" both love and hate the same object; they "naturally" entertain different desires subconsciously than consciously. In civilized times men have learned to control to some extent their irrational impulses, in the interest of adjusting to the social environment in which they live. In acquiring socially-acceptable patterns of behavior, some impulses are discouraged while others are encouraged. Even so, in their "emotions," which account for much human behavior, men are "naturally" ambivalent. Loyalty and disloyalty, courage and cowardice, generosity and selfishness, affection and hatred—all are bases of political behavior. In fact, on such non-rational emotions many of our accepted political beliefs and practices rest.

In the light of advances made during the past half-century in psychological studies, Wallas' theory leaves much wanting. Since his book was first published, major psychological schools like Behaviorism, Gestalt, and Freudian psychology have developed. Even the concept of "human nature" has virtually disappeared from the literature of contemporary psychology. Wallas was keenly aware of the shortcomings of his theory, and in the course of his lifetime he modified it. But his main contention remains undisturbed: empirical psychological findings show that the theory of human nature entertained by the Benthamites is unrealistic. The view that human action can be explained in terms of the rational pursuit of self-interest in happiness is much too simple. At best it is a misleading half-truth. What we can glean from Wallas' critique is that the Benthamite psychology entails two significant weaknesses. One is that reason is not the guide for all political actions; emotions account for many. The other is that "happiness" is not the only goal men desire; it is one of many conflicting goals which men are emotionally stirred to seek. The Benthamite psychological assumptions, then, afford no firm basis for a political theory.

VII

One legitimate test for evaluating a political theory, and especially a theory in which a premium is put on "reason," is that of logical coherence. Are the contentions advanced in the theory logically consistent? Utilitarianism is most significantly a theory of social ethics, designed to prescribe how men should act. But it is a theory which suffers some unresolved logical difficulties.

It is one thing to proclaim rules men should live by, and quite another to justify the rules. The moralist is always confronted with the task of showing *why* men should follow rules of right conduct. Medieval Christian moralists faced up to this task in a frank fashion. They contended that the universe is ordered by natural laws defining right and wrong conduct. Men should act according to these laws because the Creator of the universe wills that His laws be obeyed by His creatures. God endowed man with a dual nature, temporal and spiritual. It is God's will that during his life on earth man seek salvation of his immortal soul. The true Christian believer knows that he must obey the laws which God wills in order to obtain salvation on the Day of Judgment; the punishment for failure to obey the rules of right conduct is eternal damnation.

The "enlightened" thinkers of the seventeenth and eighteenth centuries repudiated religious faith as grounds for beliefs about this world. Characteristically they founded their political theories on assumptions of laws of nature, too, but they took their natural laws to be self-evidently true. The doctrines of natural rights and of social contract were based on secular natural law assumptions. But with these theories there is a difficulty. Natural laws are taken by such thinkers to be prescriptive of how men *should* act, as well as descriptive of how they *do* act. Why should men act differently than they "naturally" do? Because "reason" so dictates, the Enlightenment thinkers answer; in such theories the "reason of man" rather than the "will of God" presumably justifies certain norms for human conduct. But why should man act rationally? The only answer provided by secular natural law theorists is, in effect, to achieve salvation of his mortal body in this world. Why *should* man seek this paradise on earth? The Enlightenment thinkers answered this question only by begging it.

The Benthamites, following David Hume, professed to repudiate natural law assumptions in propounding their theory of ethics. Bentham branded "natural rights" as a fiction; he referred to the "social contract" as "nonsense on stilts." Utility was taken to be the universal norm for right conduct. Yet Utilitarianism is on close inspection intelligible only in terms of certain natural law assumptions which bear a strong family resemblance to those entertained by the natural rights-social contract thinkers of the Enlightenment.

For example: Why should the government promote the greatest happiness of the greatest number? Because all individuals seek happiness. But *should* the interests of individuals in happiness be considered equally? Yes, the Benthamite answers: "each should count for one and no more than one." But why? There can be only one answer: each and every individual has a natural right to happiness. Without this tacit assumption, the whole Utilitarian theory falls apart. Yet it is assumed that nature, not men, decrees the law that each man has a right to happiness.

Another less obvious example in Utilitarian theory is the natural law assumption underlying the identification of individual happiness with the greatest happiness; the sums of individual interests are assumed to be equivalent to the social interest. Of course, in practice individual self-interest does conflict with the interests of others; the majority's happiness is apt to be at the expense of the minority's interests. The Benthamites dismissed this difficulty by the claim that the conflict is apparent, not real. There is no conflict between individual interest and the social interest *provided men act rationally*. This is called the principle of artificial identification of interests. Utility means both the greatest happiness of the individual and the greatest happiness of the greatest number, but both rationally perceived. If every individual pursues his self-interest rationally in accord with the principle of utility, the Benthamite holds that the social interest is then automatically promoted.

Perhaps so. But if every individual acted rationally there would also be no need for a Utilitarian theory prescribing how men should act to achieve happiness. The point is that in practice men do not always act rationally; of course the Benthamite recognizes that this is the case by claiming that men *should* act according to the principle of utility. The practical question, then, is: *Who* should determine, in accord with the principle of utility, how men should act? The common individual in whom the light of reason flickers faintly cannot determine the utility of an act. For the same reason the vote of the greater number of individuals, the most expedient device for resolving differences among a group of persons, cannot be determining. So the Benthamite is confronted by a curious dilemma: The people know what they want if you don't ask them, but they don't know what they want if you do.[9]

A difficulty with this Utilitarian theory of ethics is that it is either logically incoherent or empirically unrealistic. The Benthamite holds that the utility of an act must be determined "scientifically," by consulting "experience," through use of "reason." The logic of this position requires that a moral judgment can be made only by those qualified to apply the principle of utility—only by "rational men." This formula is meaningful provided certain natural law assumptions are accepted. In holding that rational men can judge the utility of an act, it must be assumed that they, unlike other men, can perceive an objective, universal standard of right and wrong. But if there is no conflict of interest in the theory, it is not simply because rational men are making the judgments. It is because the standard prescribes a harmony of interests. To avoid conflict of interest, it must be assumed that the laws ordering the nature of human relations command harmony, and that men ought to act in conformity with these laws. Granted these assumptions, the Benthamite formula for identifying the greatest happiness of the individual with the greatest happiness of the greatest number is at least intelligible. Only by appeal to such natural law principles is the Utilitarian theory made coherent.

However, this is slight consolation for the dedicated Benthamite. Because he ostensibly refuses to accept laws of nature as norms for human conduct, he is confronted, as the secular natural-law theorist is confronted, with unresolved logical difficulties in his theory. Yet his refusal to accept natural law principles is quite understandable. It is unrealistic to contend that men should guide their conduct by certain rules when

[9] In his essay on "Liberty of the Press" James Mill attempted to avoid this difficulty by holding that the vote of the greatest number should determine, on the grounds that the majority is more likely to judge right than the minority. But Mill meant, as we shall see, the majority of "rational men"; in his view the greater number of people were not even qualified to exercise the franchise, let alone to judge a moral question.

there is no adequate way to resolve disagreements about what
the rules actually prescribe. On questions of natural rights,
nature remains mute; it is men suffering human frailty who
debate. In practice different persons relying on the same
natural law principles disagree violently in judging the
morality of conduct. Of course, one could abandon the quest
for a logic of morals and hold that differences about matters of
conduct should be resolved by the vote of the majority,
through the democratic process of group decision-making.
This would be a realistic method for resolving such differences. But one would at the same time have to abandon the
principle of utility, certainly a drastic move for a Utilitarian.

VIII

With a theory founded on such inadequate and unrealistic
assumptions, the Benthamites were understandably faced with
immense practical difficulties when trying to apply their
Utilitarian principles. In fact the difficulties proved so serious
that the movement was finally split apart. But these difficulties
did not prevent the Utilitarians from influencing nineteenth-
century British life in a most profound fashion. Guided by
James Mill's dogmas, the Utilitarians agitated for political
reforms, with the aim of establishing a system of representative government under which individuals could pursue their
self-interests without restraint. To a remarkable extent the
Utilitarians achieved this aim.

Utilitarianism played such a vital historical role because it
served as the creed of the British middle class. That class was
produced by developments associated with the Industrial
Revolution. In Mill's day the middle-class members of British
society made their fortunes in trade, manufacture, and the
professions. They exhibited impressive wealth and talent; they
were prosperous and well-educated. But they enjoyed scant
social prestige or political influence. British society was then
dominated by the aristocracy whose wealth consisted in land.
Their rights were derived from birth and rested on custom,

not individual merit. Their privileged status was sanctioned by the Church and guaranteed by the law. An elaborate system of controls over the economic, political, social, and religious lives of the citizens enforced inequalities among members of British society.

It was this system, by which governmental authority was used to secure the privileges of a favored few, that the Benthamites sought to discredit when they addressed themselves to the question of the proper relation between the individual and authority. Government, they declared, is a means to the end of individual happiness. Law is contingent on the satisfaction of individual interests. Authority should be used only to promote the greatest happiness of the greatest number of individuals. The provident, intelligent, industrious, talented individuals should be free to seek their happiness, unhampered by government.

Consequently it was in the interest of emancipating the middle class that the Benthamites demanded extensive reforms in British life. For them reform meant, understandably, removing governmental controls over individuals; it meant *repealing* laws, not *enacting* them. In their enthusiasm to discredit the system sanctioning aristocratic privileges, the Benthamites tended to deprecate government authority in exalting the liberty of individuals. Indeed this tendency was encouraged by the Utilitarian tenets.

Granted the Benthamite theory of human nature, the field of action wherein legislation is appropriate is narrowly restricted. "All government," Bentham once wrote, "is itself a vast evil." Legislation entails imposing punishment. Punishment, which means for some individuals pain, is a necessary but undesirable instrument for achieving a goal, and should be imposed only for the sake of avoiding greater pain—more unhappiness for more people. Therefore, legislation is not warranted if there is no "mischief" to prevent. It is not warranted if the mischief cannot be effectively prevented by means of law. It is not warranted if the law will result in more mischief, in the form of secondary consequences, than it would prevent. A governor should legislate only when he *knows* what yields the greatest happiness. Laws contrary to human nature, laws which fail to promote the greatest happiness, therefore, should be repealed. In short, legislation should be kept to a bare minimum.

In the hands of the Benthamites the test of utility, as a result, provided scant grounds for justifying any law. Yet it supplied ample grounds for opposing legislation. Relying on this test, James Mill contended that the function of government should be restricted to protecting private property. Only by intervening to prevent one individual from violating the property of another does government promote the greatest happiness.

Thanks to their reform efforts, the Utilitarians' beliefs and practices were gradually incorporated to a marked degree into nineteenth-century British life. The social and political influence of the merchant, manufacturer, and professional groups did increase, to match their economic position. The influence of the landed aristocracy did decline under the onslaughts of middle-class reform. Victorian England was a fine tribute to the success of the Utilitarian movement.

But time played an ironic trick on the Utilitarians. The success of their creed paved the way for the decline of middle-class influence. James Mill and his cohorts assumed that the greatest happiness of the greatest number is always equivalent to the interests of the middle class. Eventually this assumption became untenable, under the pressure of novel circumstances.

During Mill's lifetime the Industrial Revolution wrought some marked changes in social and economic affairs, but the full impact of industrial capitalism was not felt in Britain until well into the century, after Utilitarian reforms had taken effect. Industrial capitalism meant a tremendously augmented capacity to produce wealth. But between the production of wealth and its distribution there was a glaring discrepancy. With individuals free to pursue their self-interests unrestrained, shocking inequality of conditions developed. Now the threat to individual happiness came not from a domineering government; it came from powerful, ruthless private interests engaged in a struggle for wealth and power. Indeed government, an instrument of middle-class rule, was relegated to the role of an armed guard, charged merely with the task of protecting the property of successful merchants and manufacturers.

But with industrial capitalism a new class appeared, the "working poor," employed in the mills and shops. While their middle-class employers were reaping huge profits from manufacture and trade, poverty was the lot of the many wage workers. They were compelled to labor long hours at low pay under miserable conditions. They were herded into urban slums where disease and vice were rampant. In the midst of vast wealth, the working class suffered chronic depression. The working class was rapidly becoming the most numerous part of the population; but because they were allowed no share of political influence, the minority middle class continued its domination.

Consequently, in the course of the century a sharp and bitter conflict of interests emerged between the politically dominant and prosperous middle class and the impoverished and politically inarticulate working class. The question of the proper relation between individual liberty and government authority changed radically in character from James Mill's day. Eventually that question became joined with the new "social question": How to improve the lot of the industrial working class? Set in the context of an industrial capitalist society, to these questions Utilitarianism provided no satisfactory answers. The theory was formulated prior to the industrialization of Britain, as a critique of an aristocratic regime. It was not designed to explain relations between members of an industrial society. It countenanced neither a wage working class nor a government actively serving the interests of the public. Hence on the important questions of the day the followers of Bentham and Mill held widely divergent views.

How can the greatest happiness of the greatest number be promoted in an industrial society where the vast majority suffer terribly from exploitation by powerful special interests? On the answer to this question the Utilitarians split into two contrary camps. Out of the Benthamite tradition came both a liberal and a socialist school.

The liberals clung to the Utilitarian means of an earlier day; they continued to advocate the old policy of laissez-faire. The only rational route to human happiness is the unrestrained pursuit of individual self-interest. Each individual should look after his own. Though a few unfortunates may suffer, in the long run everything will work out for the best of all concerned if government doesn't interfere in private affairs.

The Utilitarians who cherished the goal of human happiness more than the policy of laissez-faire stressed collective action in the interest of the working class. Robert Owen, the first man to call himself a socialist, imbued with Utilitarian dogma, was a foremost exponent of collectivism. Society should be ordered for the benefit of the greatest number, not the few. Individuals should associate for the purpose of promoting their common interests.

But what sort of collective action is proper? What all Utilitarians, liberal and socialist, shared was a conviction that government is an unfit instrument for remedying social and economic ills. Historically the entire thrust of Benthamite reforms had been against government controls over individuals. So we find the middle-class reformers sponsoring *private* collective action as the method for achieving their social goals, avoiding government action. During the second quarter of the nineteenth century varied collectivist experiments were undertaken by social reformers. One approach was to try to restore a pre-industrial system of production and consumption by having farming and manufacture balanced at the village level; the utopian communities were a consequence of this approach. Another was to try to make the workers self-employed, eliminating the capitalist employer; producer co-operatives and labor exchanges were results. One approach was to try to stretch out the meager incomes of wage workers so that more goods and services could be acquired from the limited resources: consumer co-operatives and benefit societies were consequences. Still another approach was to try to organize the workers for collective action in dealing with employers for the purpose of improving wages, hours, and working conditions; the trade-union movement was the ultimate product.

These many "direct action" collectivist experiments undertaken to improve the lot of the working class all failed, however. With the methods advocated by middle-class social reformers the working-class leaders became disillusioned. Finally they took a leaf from the Utilitarian notebook: they sought political power for the working class as the step toward achieving social and economic reforms.

This working-class aspiration was expressed during the 1840's by the Chartist movement. The 1832 reform gave the franchise to prosperous members of the middle class but the high property-holding qualifications for voting excluded virtually all working-class members. The main aim of the Chartists was to extend to the working class the privileges enjoyed by the middle class as a result of the 1832 reform.

Though Francis Place was an active Chartist leader, generally speaking, the followers of Utilitarianism vigorously opposed the movement. What support the Chartists received from the political leaders of the day came from the Tories. Unlike the Utilitarians, the Tories had no traditional aversion to the use of government authority to achieve social goals. They were prepared to enact legislation benefiting the underprivileged majority; what social legislation was passed in the nineteenth century, prior to the rise of the Labour Party, resulted from Tory efforts. And it was the Tory democrats who, in 1867, first gave the vote to members of the working class, over the bitter opposition of middle-class liberals.

In their hostility to the Chartist movement, and generally in their resistance to democratic reforms, the Utilitarian liberals revealed their rank class prejudice. The authority of the British Government was used to crush the Chartist movement and other movements of popular protest against the privileges of the wealthy few. The liberals regarded it as quite proper for government to be used to protect middle-class property, but not to preserve working-class lives.

The Utilitarian line to secure domination by the aristocracy of wealth was laid down by James Mill in the essay on "Government." Though passages of his essay may appear to justify the exercise of political power by the "lower orders," Mill actually took great pains to justify limiting political rights to the "wise and virtuous members of society, the middle rank." The basis for exclusion of the majority of citizens was, characteristically enough, the test of "reason."

Mill argues that only persons capable of rational action should possess political power. The suffrage should be granted to those individuals able to judge rationally their self-interest. Of course, children cannot do this, nor can women, but then their interests are secured by fathers and husbands. Only adult males, age forty, with a substantial amount of property, qualify; age and wealth are evidence of suitable "rationality." Anyway, members of the working class, poor and illiterate, do not really understand what is to their best interests. They should be guided by their betters, the reputable members of the middle class, who have clearly demonstrated their competence for rational pursuit of self-interest. They, and only they, can be relied on to take care of the greatest happiness. Bluntly put, the wealthy minority should rule the entire society.[10]

---

[10] In an article published a decade before the essay on "Government," Mill quotes with approval the maxim "that as much as possible should be done *for* the people—but nothing *by* them," and he argues that the danger of a wide base of representation is that "you incur the inconveniences of the ignorant and precipitate passions of the vulgar." From "Emancipation of Spanish America," *Edinburgh Review*, Vol. 13 (Jan., 1809), pp. 277-311.

But the theory that had proved so effective in undermining the privileges of the landed aristocracy proved quite ineffective in securing middle-class privileges. Eventually the elite rule of the wealthy minority gave way to the democratic rule of the common man in Great Britain. Then, thanks to the Tory democrats and the reconstructed liberals who had abandoned their middle-class prejudices, the authority of the British Government was used to promote the greatest happiness of the greatest number of subjects through social and economic legislation. Later the British Socialists expanded and improved such legislation, using the democratic process of representative government as a means to the end of greater human happiness.

IX

Whatever the shortcomings of the Utilitarian political theory, and notably of the views Mill expounds in his essay on "Government," it remains that Utilitarianism did exert a profound influence on nineteenth-century British thought and practice. Members of Mill's circle, all of whom had mastered the much-discussed principles of his essay, were—as publicists, agitators, and politicians—active leaders of the movement culminating in the Reform of 1832, which presaged the decline of the aristocracy and the rise of the middle class to political influence. Many ideas propagated by the Benthamites were reformulated and incorporated into other political creeds. But when Utilitarianism played out its historic role of eroding away the beliefs and practices on which the privileges of the landed aristocracy rested, it ceased to be a creed of radical reform; it became a creed of middle-class reaction. Then Utilitarianism became outmoded, and the political theory propounded by James Mill passed into political oblivion. Though this theory is now virtually dead, unlike so many ingenious concoctions by political thinkers, Mill's theory at least lived. In the words of his biographer, Alexander Bain, the publication of the essay on "Government" marked "an epoch in the political history of the time." Few political writings have left such an imprint on the life of an age as the remarkable essay you find reprinted on the following pages.

CURRIN V. SHIELDS

University of California,
  Los Angeles

June 30, 1955

SELECTED BIBLIOGRAPHY

I

James Mill's principal works and his shorter writings of some political significance are listed below:

The History of British India. 3 vols., 1817; 2nd ed., 6 vols., 1820; London: Baldwin, Craddock & Joy. 5th ed., 10 vols., with notes and continuation by Horace H. Wilson; London: J. Madden, 1856.

Elements of Political Economy. 1821; 2nd ed., 1824; 3rd ed., 1826, revised and corrected; London: Baldwin, Craddock & Joy.

Analysis of the Phenomena of the Human Mind. 2 vols.; London: Baldwin & Craddock, 1829. New ed., 2 vols., edited with notes by J. S. Mill and with notes illustrative and critical by Alexander Bain, Andrew Findlater, and George Grote; London: Longmans, Green, Reader & Dyer, 1869.

A Fragment on Mackintosh: Being Strictures on Some Passages in the Dissertation by Sir James Mackintosh prefixed to the Encyclopaedia Britannica. 1835; 2nd ed., 1870; London: Baldwin & Craddock.

"Money and Exchange." *Edinburgh Review,* Vol. 13 (Oct., 1808), pp. 35-68.

"Emancipation of Spanish America." *Edinburgh Review,* Vol. 13 (Jan., 1809), pp. 277-311.

"Bexon's Code." *Edinburgh Review,* Vol. 15 (Oct., 1809), pp. 88-109.

"Napoleonic Code." *Edinburgh Review,* Vol. 17 (Nov., 1810), pp. 88-114.

"Education of the Poor." *Edinburgh Review,* Vol. 21 (Feb., 1813), pp. 207-219.

"Education" (1818); "Government" (1819); "Jurisprudence" (1819); "Liberty of the Press" (1821). Supplement to the Fifth Edition of the *Encyclopaedia Britannica.*

"Edinburgh Review." *Westminster Review,* Vol. 1 (Jan., 1824), pp. 206-249.

"Quarterly Review." *Westminster Review,* Vol. 2 (Oct., 1824), pp. 463-503.

"Southey's Book of the Church." *Westminster Review,* Vol. 3 (Jan., 1825), pp. 167-213.

"Formation and Publication of Opinions." *Westminster Review,* Vol. 6 (July, 1826), pp. 1-23.

"State of the Nation." *Westminster Review,* Vol. 6 (Oct., 1826), pp. 249-278.

"The Ballot." *Westminster Review,* Vol. 13 (July, 1830), pp. 1-39.

II

James Mill and Utilitarianism are subjects of the important and useful works listed below:

Alexander Bain, *James Mill: A Biography.* London: Longmans, Green & Co., 1882.

George S. Bower, *David Hartley and James Mill.* New York: Putnam's Sons, 1881.

William L. Davidson, *Political Thought in England: the Utilitarians from Bentham to J. S. Mill.* New York: Holt & Co., 1916.

Élie Halévy, *The Growth of Philosophical Radicalism.* Translated by Mary Morris; with a preface by A. D. Lindsay. London: Faber & Faber, Ltd., 1949.

Mark Hovell, *The Chartist Movement.* Edited by T. F. Tout. Manchester: Manchester University, 1918.

John Stuart Mill, *Autobiography.* Preface by J. J. Coss. New York: Columbia University Press, 1924.

Emery Neff, *Carlyle and Mill, Mystic and Utilitarian.* New York: Columbia University Press, 1926.

George L. Nesbitt, *Benthamite Reviewing: The First Twelve Years of the Westminster Review, 1824-1836.* New York: Columbia University Press, 1934.

John Petrov Plamenatz, *The English Utilitarians.* Oxford: Blackwell, 1949.

Leslie Stephens, *The English Utilitarians.* 3 vols.; London: Duckworth & Co., 1900. (Vol. II is devoted to James Mill.)

Graham Wallas, *The Life of Francis Place, 1771-1854.* Revised ed.; London: G. Allen & Unwin, Ltd., 1918.

George Malcolm Young, *Victorian England, Portrait of an Age.* 2nd ed.; London: Oxford University Press, 1953.

NOTE ON THE TEXT

This essay on *Government* was published as a Supplement to the Fifth Edition of the *Encyclopaedia Britannica* and later published in book form for the first time by J. Innes, apparently under the supervision of the author.

The present edition follows the Innes edition with the exception of the paragraphing. Spelling and punctuation have been revised throughout to conform to current American usage.

AN ESSAY ON GOVERNMENT

I

THE END OF GOVERNMENT; VIZ., THE GOOD OR BENEFIT FOR THE SAKE OF WHICH IT EXISTS

THE QUESTION with respect to government is a question about the adaptation of means to an end. Notwithstanding the portion of discourse which has been bestowed upon this subject, it is surprising to find, on a close inspection, how few of its principles are settled. The reason is that the ends and means have not been analyzed, and it is only a general and undistinguishing conception of them which is found in the minds of the greatest number of men. Things in this situation give rise to interminable disputes; more especially when the deliberation is subject, as here, to the strongest action of personal interest.

In a discourse limited as the present, it would be obviously vain to attempt the accomplishment of such a task as that of the analysis we have mentioned. The mode, however, in which the operation should be conducted may perhaps be described, and evidence enough exhibited to show in what road we must travel to approach the goal at which so many have vainly endeavored to arrive.

The end of government has been described in a great variety of expressions. By Locke it was said to be "the public good"; by others it has been described as being "the greatest happiness of the greatest number." These, and equivalent expressions, are just; but they are defective inasmuch as the particular ideas which they embrace are indistinctly announced, and different conceptions are by means of them raised in different minds, and even in the same mind on different occasions.

It is immediately obvious that a wide and difficult field is presented, and that the whole science of human nature must be explored to lay a foundation for the science of government. To understand what is included in the happiness of the greatest number, we must understand what is included in the happiness of the individuals of whom it is composed. That dissection of human nature which would be necessary for exhibiting, on proper evidence, the primary elements into which human happiness may be resolved, it is not compatible with the present design to undertake. We must content ourselves with assuming certain results.

We may allow, for example, in general terms that the lot of every human being is determined by his pains and pleasures, and that his happiness corresponds with the degree in which his pleasures are great and his pains are small. Human pains and pleasures are derived from two sources: they are produced either by our fellow men or by causes independent of other men. We may assume it as another principle that the concern of government is with the former of these two sources: that its business is to increase to the utmost the pleasures, and diminish to the utmost the pains, which men derive from one another.

Of the laws of nature on which the condition of man depends, that which is attended with the greatest number of consequences is the necessity of labor for obtaining the means of subsistence as well as the means of the greatest part of our pleasures. This is no doubt the primary cause of government; for if nature had produced spontaneously all the objects which we desire, and in sufficient abundance for the desires of all, there would have been no source of dispute or of injury among men, nor would any man have possessed the means of ever acquiring authority over another.

The results are exceedingly different when nature produces the objects of desire not in sufficient abundance for all. The source of dispute is then exhaustless, and every man has the means of acquiring authority over others in proportion to the quantity of those objects which he is able to possess. In this case the end to be obtained through government as the means is to make that distribution of the scanty materials of happiness which would insure the greatest sum of it in the members of the community taken altogether, preventing every individual or combination of individuals from interfering with that distribution or making any man to have less than his share.

When it is considered that most of the objects of desire and even the means of subsistence are the product of labor, it is evident that the means of insuring labor must be provided for as the foundation of all. The means for the insuring of labor are of two sorts: the one made out of the matter of evil, the other made out of the matter of good. The first sort is commonly denominated "force," and under its application the laborers are slaves. This mode of procuring labor we need not consider, for if the end of government be to produce the greatest happiness of the greatest number, that end cannot be attained by making the greatest number slaves.

The other mode of obtaining labor is by allurement, or the advantage which it brings. To obtain all the objects of desire in the greatest possible quantity, we must obtain labor in the greatest possible quantity; and to obtain labor in the greatest possible quantity, we must raise to the greatest possible height the advantage attached to labor. It is impossible to attach to labor a greater degree of advantage than the whole of the product of labor. Why so? Because if you give more to one man than the produce of his labor, you can do so only by taking it away from the produce of some other man's labor. The greatest possible happiness of society is, therefore, attained by insuring to every man the greatest possible quantity of the produce of his labor.

How is this to be accomplished? For it is obvious that every man who has not all the objects of his desire has inducement to take them from any other man who is weaker than himself: and how is he to be prevented? One mode is sufficiently obvious, and it does not appear that there is any other: the union of a certain number of men to protect one another. The object, it is plain, can best be attained when a great number of men combine and delegate to a small number the power necessary for protecting them all. This is government.

With respect to the end of government, or that for the sake of which it exists, it is not conceived to be necessary on the present occasion that the analysis should be carried any further. What follows is an attempt to analyze the means.

II

THE MEANS OF ATTAINING THE END OF GOVERNMENT; VIZ., POWER, AND SECURITIES AGAINST THE ABUSE OF THAT POWER

Two things are here to be considered: the power with which the small number are entrusted, and the use which they are to make of it. With respect to the first there is no difficulty. The elements out of which the power of coercing others is fabricated are obvious to all. Of these we shall therefore not lengthen this article by any explanation. All the difficult questions of government relate to the means of restraining those in whose hands are lodged the powers necessary for the protection of all from making bad use of it.

Whatever would be the temptations under which individuals would lie if there was no government, to take the objects of desire from others weaker than themselves, under the same temptations the members of government lie to take the objects of desire from the members of the community if they are not prevented from doing so. Whatever, then, are the reasons for establishing government, the very same exactly are the reasons for establishing securities that those entrusted with the powers necessary for protecting others make use of them for that purpose solely, and not for the purpose of taking from the members of the community the objects of desire.

III

THAT THE REQUISITE SECURITIES AGAINST THE ABUSE OF POWER ARE NOT FOUND IN ANY OF THE SIMPLE FORMS OF GOVERNMENT

THERE are three modes in which it may be supposed that the powers for the protection of the community are capable of being exercised. The community may undertake the protection of itself and of its members. The powers of protection may be placed in the hands of a few. And, lastly, they may be placed in the hands of an individual. The many, the few, the one: these varieties appear to exhaust the subject. It is not possible to conceive any hands or combination of hands in which the powers of protection can be lodged, which will not fall under one or other of those descriptions. And these varieties correspond to the three forms of government: the democratical, the aristocratical, and the monarchical. It will be necessary to look somewhat closely at each of these forms in their order.

(1) *The democratical.* It is obviously impossible that the community in a body can be present to afford protection to each of its members. It must employ individuals for that purpose. Employing individuals, it must choose them; it must lay down the rules under which they are to act; and it must punish them if they act in disconformity to those rules. In these functions are included the three great operations of government: administration, legislation, and judicature. The community, to perform any of these operations, must be assembled. This circumstance alone seems to form a conclusive objection against the democratical form. To assemble the whole of a community as often as the business of government requires performance would almost preclude the existence of labor, hence that of property, and hence the existence of the community itself.

There is another objection, not less conclusive. A whole

community would form a numerous assembly. But all numerous assemblies are essentially incapable of business. It is unnecessary to be tedious in the proof of this proposition. In an assembly everything must be done by speaking and assenting. But where the assembly is numerous, so many persons desire to speak, and feelings by mutual inflammation become so violent, that calm and effectual deliberation is impossible.

It may be taken, therefore, as a position from which there will be no dissent, that a community in mass is ill-adapted for the business of government. There is no principle more in conformity with the sentiments and the practice of the people than this. The management of the joint affairs of any considerable body of the people they never undertake for themselves. What they uniformly do is to choose a certain number of themselves to be the actors in their stead. Even in the case of a common benefit club, the members choose a committee of management and content themselves with a general control.

(2) *The aristocratical.*   This term applies to all those cases in which the powers of government are held by any number of persons intermediate between a single person and the majority. When the number is small, it is common to call the government an oligarchy; when it is considerable, to call it an aristocracy. The cases are essentially the same, because the motives which operate in both are the same. This is a proposition which carries, we think, its own evidence along with it. We, therefore, assume it as a point which will not be disputed.

The source of evil is radically different in the case of aristocracy from what it is in that of democracy.

The community cannot have an interest opposite to its interest. To affirm this would be a contradiction in terms. The community within itself, and with respect to itself, can have no sinister interest. One community may intend the evil of another; never its own. This is an indubitable proposition, and one of great importance. The community may act wrong from mistake. To suppose that it could from design, would be to suppose that human beings can wish their own misery.

The circumstances from which the inaptitude of the community, as a body, for the business of government arises—namely, the inconvenience of assembling them, and the inconvenience of their numbers when assembled—do not necessarily exist in the case of aristocracy. If the number of those who hold among them the powers of government is so great as to make it inconvenient to assemble them, or impossible for them to deliberate calmly when assembled, this is only an objection to so extended an aristocracy and has no application to an aristocracy not too numerous, when assembled, for the best exercise of deliberation.

The question is whether such an aristocracy may be trusted to make that use of the powers of government which is most conducive to the end for which government exists?

There may be a strong presumption that any aristocracy monopolizing the powers of government would not possess intellectual powers in any very high perfection. Intellectual powers are the offspring of labor. But a hereditary aristocracy are deprived of the strongest motives to labor. The greater part of them will, therefore, be defective in those mental powers. This is one objection, and an important one, though not the greatest.

We have already observed that the reason for which government exists is that one man, if stronger than another, will take from him whatever that other possesses and he desires. But if one man will do this, so will several. And if powers are put into the hands of a comparatively small number, called an aristocracy—powers which make them stronger than the rest of the community—they will take from the rest of the community as much as they please of the objects of desire. They will thus defeat the very end for which government was instituted. The unfitness, therefore, of an aristocracy to be entrusted with the powers of government rests on demonstration.

(3) *The monarchical.* It will be seen, and therefore words to make it manifest are unnecessary, that in most respects the monarchical form of government agrees with the aristocratical

and is liable to the same objections. If government is founded
upon this, as a law of human nature, that a man if able will
take from others anything which they have and he desires,
it is sufficiently evident that when a man is called a king it
does not change his nature; so that when he has got power
to enable him to take from every man what he pleases, he
will take whatever he pleases. To suppose that he will not is
to affirm that government is unnecessary and that human
beings will abstain from injuring one another of their own
accord.

It is very evident that this reasoning extends to every modification of the smaller number. Whenever the powers of government are placed in any hands other than those of the
community—whether those of one man, of a few, or of several—those principles of human nature which imply that
government is at all necessary imply that those persons will
make use of them to defeat the very end for which government exists.

IV

AN OBJECTION STATED—AND ANSWERED

ONE observation, however, suggests itself. Allowing, it may
be said, that this deduction is perfect and the inference
founded upon it indisputable, it is yet true that, if there were
no government, every man would be exposed to depredation
from every man; but under an aristocracy he is exposed to it
only from a few, under a monarchy only from one. This is a
highly important objection, and deserves to be minutely investigated.

It is sufficiently obvious that if every man is liable to be deprived of what he possesses at the will of every man stronger
than himself, the existence of property is impossible; and if
the existence of property is impossible, so also is that of labor,
of the means of subsistence for an enlarged community, and
hence of the community itself. If the members of such a com-

munity are liable to deprivation by only a few hundred men, the members of an aristocracy, it may not be impossible to satiate that limited number with a limited portion of the objects belonging to all. Allowing this view of the subject to be correct, it follows that the smaller the number of hands into which the powers of government are permitted to pass, the happier it will be for the community: that an oligarchy, therefore, is better than an aristocracy, and a monarchy better than either.

This view of the subject deserves to be the more carefully considered because the conclusion to which it leads is the same with that which has been adopted and promulgated by some of the most profound and most benevolent investigators of human affairs. That government by one man, altogether unlimited and uncontrolled, is better than government by any modification of aristocracy is the celebrated opinion of Mr. Hobbes and of the French *économistes,* supported on reasonings which it is not easy to controvert. Government by the many they with reason considered an impossibility. They inferred, therefore, that of all the possible forms of government absolute monarchy is the best.

Experience, if we look only at the outside of the facts, appears to be divided on this subject. Absolute monarchy under Neros and Caligulas, under such men as emperors of Morocco and sultans of Turkey, is the scourge of human nature. On the other side, the people of Denmark, tired out with the oppression of an aristocracy, resolved that their king should be absolute, and under their absolute monarch are as well governed as any people in Europe. In Greece, notwithstanding the defects of democracy, human nature ran a more brilliant career than it has ever done in any other age or country. As the surface of history affords, therefore, no certain principle of decision, we must go beyond the surface and penetrate to the springs within.

When it is said that one man or a limited number of men will soon be satiated with the objects of desire and, when they have taken from the community what suffices to satiate them, will protect its members in the enjoyment of the remainder, an important element of the calculation is left out. Human beings are not a passive substance. If human beings in respect to their rulers were the same as sheep in respect to their shepherd, and if the king or the aristocracy were as totally exempt from all fear of resistance from the people, and all chance of obtaining more obedience from severity, as the shepherd in the case of the sheep, it does appear that there would be a limit to the motive for taking to one's self the objects of desire. The case will be found to be very much altered when the idea is taken into the account, first, of the resistance to his will which one human being may expect from another, and secondly, of that perfection in obedience which fear alone can produce.

That one human being will desire to render the person and property of another subservient to his pleasures, notwithstanding the pain or loss of pleasure which it may occasion to that other individual, is the foundation of government. The desire of the object implies the desire of the power necessary to accomplish the object. The desire, therefore, of that power which is necessary to render the persons and properties of human beings subservient to our pleasures is a grand governing law of human nature. What is implied in that desire of power, and what is the extent to which it carries the actions of men, are the questions which it is necessary to resolve in order to discover the limit which nature has set to the desire on the part of a king or an aristocracy to inflict evil upon the community for their own advantage.

Power is a means to an end. The end is everything, without exception, which the human being calls pleasure and the removal of pain. The grand instrument for attaining what a man likes is the actions of other men. Power in its most appropriate signification, therefore, means security for the conformity between the will of one man and the acts of other men. This, we presume, is not a proposition which will be disputed. The master has power over his servant, because when he wills him to do so and so—in other words, expresses a desire that he would do so and so—he possesses a kind of security that the actions of the man will correspond to his desire. The general commands his soldiers to perform certain operations, the king commands his subjects to act in a certain manner, and their power is complete or not complete in proportion as the conformity is complete or not complete between the actions willed and the actions performed. The actions of other men, considered as means for the attainment of the objects of our desire, are perfect or imperfect in proportion as they are or are not certainly and invariably correspondent to our will. There is no limit, therefore, to the demand of security for the perfection of that correspondence. A man is never satisfied with a smaller degree if he can obtain a greater. And as there is no man whatsoever whose acts, in some degree or other, in some way or other, more immediately or more remotely, may not have some influence as means to our ends, there is no man the conformity of whose acts to our will we would not give something to secure. The demand, therefore, of power over the acts of other men is really boundless. It is boundless in two ways: boundless in the number of persons to whom we would extend it, and boundless in its degree over the actions of each.

It would be nugatory to say, with a view to explain away this important principle, that some human beings may be so remotely connected with our interests as to make the desire of a conformity between our will and their actions evanescent. It is quite enough to assume, what nobody will deny, that our desire of that conformity is unlimited in respect to all those men whose actions can be supposed to have any influence on our pains and pleasures. With respect to the rulers of a community this at least is certain, that they have a desire for the conformity between their will and the actions of every man in the community. And for our present purpose this is as wide a field as we need to embrace.

With respect to the community, then, we deem it an established truth that the rulers, one or a few, desire an exact conformity between their will and the acts of every member of the community. It remains for us to inquire to what description of acts it is the nature of this desire to give existence.

There are two classes of means by which the conformity between the will of one man and the acts of other men may be accomplished. The one is pleasure, the other pain.

With regard to securities of the pleasurable sort for obtaining a conformity between one man's will and the acts of other men, it is evident from experience that when a man possesses a command over the objects of desire he may, by imparting those objects to other men, insure to a great extent conformity between his will and their actions. It follows, and is also matter of experience, that the greater the quantity of the objects of desire which he may thus impart to other men, the greater is the number of men between whose actions and his own will he can insure a conformity. As it has been demonstrated that there is no limit to the number of men whose actions we desire to have conformable to our will, it follows with equal evidence that there is no limit to the command which we desire to possess over the objects which insure this result.

It is, therefore, not true that there is in the mind of a king, or in the minds of an aristocracy, any point of saturation with the objects of desire. The opinion, in examination of which we have gone through the preceding analysis, that a king or an aristocracy may be satiated with the objects of desire and, after being satiated, leave to the members of the community the greater part of what belongs to them, is an opinion founded upon a partial and incomplete view of the laws of human nature.

We have next to consider the securities of the painful sort which may be employed for attaining conformity between the acts of one man and the will of another. We are of opinion that the importance of this part of the subject has not been duly considered and that the business of government will be ill-understood till its numerous consequences have been fully developed.

Pleasure appears to be a feeble instrument of obedience in

comparison with pain. It is much more easy to despise pleasure than pain. Above all, it is important to consider that in this class of instruments is included the power of taking away life, and with it of taking away not only all the pleasures of reality but, what goes so far beyond them, all the pleasures of hope. This class of securities is, therefore, incomparably the strongest. He who desires obedience to a high degree of exactness cannot be satisfied with the power of giving pleasure, he must have the power of inflicting pain. He who desires it to the highest possible degree of exactness must desire power of inflicting pain sufficient at least to insure that degree of exactness—that is, an unlimited power of inflicting pain; for as there is no possible mark by which to distinguish what is sufficient and what is not, and as the human mind sets no bounds to its avidity for the securities of what it deems eminently good, it is sure to extend beyond almost any limits its desire of the power of giving pain to others.

It may, however, be said that how inseparable a part soever of human nature it may appear to be to desire to possess unlimited power of inflicting pain upon others, it does not follow that those who possess it will have a desire to make use of it. This is the next part of the inquiry upon which we have to enter, and we need not add that it merits all the attention of those who would possess correct ideas upon a subject which involves the greatest interests of mankind.

The chain of inference in this case is close and strong to a most unusual degree. A man desires that the actions of other men shall be instantly and accurately correspondent to his will. He desires that the actions of the greatest possible number shall be so. Terror is the grand instrument. Terror can work only through assurance that evil will follow any want of conformity between the will and the actions willed. Every failure must therefore be punished. As there are no bounds to the mind's desire of its pleasure, there are of course no bounds to its desire of perfection in the instruments of that pleasure. There are, therefore, no bounds to its desire of exactness in the conformity between its will and the actions willed, and, by consequence, to the strength of that terror which is its procuring cause. Every, the most minute, failure must be visited with the heaviest infliction; and as failure in extreme exactness must frequently happen, the occasions of cruelty must be incessant.

We have thus arrived at several conclusions of the highest possible importance. We have seen that the very principle of human nature upon which the necessity of government is founded—the propensity of one man to possess himself of the objects of desire at the cost of another—leads on, by infallible sequence, where power over a community is attained and nothing checks, not only to that degree of plunder which leaves the members (excepting always the recipients and instruments of the plunder) the bare means of subsistence, but to that degree of cruelty which is necessary to keep in existence the most intense terror.

The world affords some decisive experiments upon human nature in exact conformity with these conclusions. An English gentleman may be taken as a favorable specimen of civilization, of knowledge, of humanity, of all the qualities, in short, that make human nature estimable. The degree in which he desires to possess power over his fellow creatures, and the degree of oppression to which he finds motives for carrying the exercise of that power, will afford a standard from which assuredly there can be no appeal. Wherever the same motives exist, the same conduct as that displayed by the English gentleman may be expected to follow in all men not further advanced in human excellence than himself. In the West Indies, before that vigilant attention of the English nation, which now for thirty years has imposed so great a check upon the masters of slaves, there was not a perfect absence of all check upon the dreadful propensities of power. But yet it is true that these propensities led English gentlemen not only to deprive their slaves of property and to make property of their fellow creatures, but to treat them with a degree of cruelty the very description of which froze the blood of those of their countrymen who were placed in less unfavorable circumstances. The motives of this deplorable conduct are exactly those which we have described above, as arising out of the universal desire to render the actions of other men exactly conformable to our will. It is of great importance to remark that not one item in the motives which led English gentlemen to make slaves of their fellow creatures and to reduce them to the very worst condition in which the Negroes have been found in the West Indies can be shown to be wanting, or to be less strong, in the set of motives which universally operate upon the men who have power over their fellow creatures. It is proved, therefore, by the closest deduction from the acknowledged laws of human nature, and by direct and decisive experiments, that the ruling *one* or the ruling *few* would, if checks did not operate in the way of prevention, reduce the great mass of the people subject to their power at least to the condition of Negroes in the West Indies.[1]

We have thus seen that of the forms of government which have been called the three simple forms, not one is adequate to the ends which government is appointed to secure; that the community itself, which alone is free from motives opposite to those ends, is incapacitated by its numbers from performing the business of government; and that, whether government is entrusted to one or a few, they have not only motives opposite to those ends, but motives which will carry them, if unchecked, to inflict the greatest evils.

These conclusions are so conformable to ordinary conceptions that it would hardly have been necessary, if the development had not been of importance for some of our subsequent investigations, to have taken any pains with the proof of them. In this country, at least, it will be remarked, in conformity with so many writers, that the imperfection of the three simple forms of government is apparent; that the ends of govern-

---

[1] An acute sense of this important truth is expressed by the President Montesquieu: "*C'est une expérience éternelle, que tout homme qui a du pouvoir est porté à en abuser; il va jusqu'à ce qu'il trouve de limites.*" —Esp. DE Loix. *L.* xi. *c.* 4. [It is an eternal experience that every man who has power is inclined to abuse it; and he will go to the very limit of it.]

ment can be attained in perfection only, as under the British constitution, by a union of all the three.

V

THAT THE REQUISITE SECURITIES ARE NOT FOUND IN A UNION OF THE THREE SIMPLE FORMS OF GOVERNMENT; DOCTRINE OF THE CONSTITUTIONAL BALANCE

THE doctrine of the union of the three simple forms of government is the next part of this important subject which we are called upon to examine.

The first thing which it is obvious to remark upon is that it has been customary, in regard to this part of the inquiry, to beg the question. The good effects which have been ascribed to the union of the three simple forms of government have been *supposed;* and the supposition has commonly been allowed. No proof has been adduced; or if anything have the appearance of proof, it has only been a reference to the British constitution. The British constitution, it has been said, is a union of the three simple forms of government; and the British government is excellent. To render the instance of the British government in any degree a proof of the doctrine in question, it is evident that three points must be established: first, that the British government is not in show, but in substance, a union of the three simple forms; secondly, that it has peculiar excellence; and, thirdly, that its excellence arises from the union so supposed, and not from any other cause. As these points have always been taken for granted without examination, the question with respect to the effects of a union of the three simple forms of government may be considered as yet unsolved.

The positions which we have already established with regard to human nature, and which we assume as foundations, are these: that the actions of men are governed by their wills, and their wills by their desires; that their desires are directed to pleasure and relief from pain as *ends,* and to wealth and power as the principal means; that to the desire of these means there is no limit; and that the actions which flow from this unlimited desire are the constituents whereof bad government is made. Reasoning correctly from these acknowledged laws of human nature, we shall presently discover what opinion, with respect to the mixture of the different species of government, it will be incumbent upon us to adopt.

The theory in question implies that, of the powers of government, one portion is held by the king, one by the aristocracy, and one by the people. It also implies that there is on the part of each of them a certain unity of will, otherwise they would not act as three separate powers. This being understood, we proceed to the inquiry.

From the principles which we have already laid down it follows that of the objects of human desire—and, speaking more definitely, of the means to the ends of human desire, namely, wealth and power—each of the three parties will endeavor to obtain as much as possible.

After what has been said, it is not suspected that any reader will deny this proposition; but it is of importance that he keep in his mind a very clear conception of it.

If any expedient presents itself to any of the supposed parties, effectual to this end and not opposed to any preferred object of pursuit, we may infer, with certainty, that it will be adopted. One effectual expedient is not more effectual than obvious. Any two of the parties, by combining, may swallow up the third. That such combination will take place appears to be as certain as anything which depends upon human will, because there are strong motives in favor of it, and none that can be conceived in opposition to it. Whether the portions of power as originally distributed to the parties be supposed to be equal or unequal, the mixture of three of the kinds of government, it is thus evident, cannot possibly exist.

This proposition appears to be so perfectly proved that we do not think it necessary to dwell here upon the subject. As a part, however, of this doctrine of the mixture of the simple forms of government it may be proper to inquire whether a union may not be possible of two of them.

Three varieties of this union may be conceived: the union of the monarchy with aristocracy, or the union of either with democracy.

Let us first suppose that monarchy is united with aristocracy. Their power is equal or not equal. If it is not equal, it follows as a necessary consequence from the principles which we have already established that the stronger will take from the weaker, till it engrosses the whole. The only question, therefore, is what will happen when the power is equal.

In the first place, it seems impossible that such equality should ever exist. How is it to be established? Or by what criterion is it to be ascertained? If there is no such criterion, it must, in all cases, be the result of chance. If so, the chances against it are as infinite to one. The idea, therefore, is wholly chimerical and absurd.

Besides, a disposition to overrate one's own advantages, and underrate those of other men, is a known law of human nature. Suppose, what would be little less than miraculous, that equality were established, this propensity would lead each of the parties to conceive itself the strongest. The consequence would be that they would go to war and contend till one or other was subdued. Either those laws of human nature, upon which all reasoning with respect to government proceeds, must be denied, and then the utility of government itself may be denied, or this conclusion is demonstrated. Again, if this equality were established, is there a human being who can suppose that it would last? If anything be known about human affairs it is this, that they are in perpetual change. If nothing else interfered, the difference of men in respect of talents would abundantly produce the effect. Suppose your equality to be established at the time when your king is a man of talents, and suppose his successor to be the reverse; your equality no longer exists. The moment one of the parties is superior, it begins to profit by its superiority, and the inequality is daily increased. It is unnecessary to extend the investigation to the remaining cases, the union of democracy with either of the other two kinds of government. It is very evident that the same reasoning would lead to the same results.

In this doctrine of the mixture of the simple forms of government is included the celebrated theory of the balance among the component parts of a government. By this it is supposed that, when a government is composed of monarchy, aristocracy, and democracy, they balance one another, and by mutual checks produce good government. A few words will suffice to show that if any theory deserve the epithets of "wild, visionary, chimerical," it is that of the balance. If there are three powers, how is it possible to prevent two of them from combining to swallow up the third?

The analysis which we have already performed will enable us to trace rapidly the concatenation of causes and effects in this imagined case.

We have already seen that the interest of the community, considered in the aggregate or in the democratical point of view, is that each individual should receive protection, and that the powers which are constituted for that purpose should be employed exclusively for that purpose. As this is a proposition wholly indisputable, it is also one to which all correct reasoning upon matters of government must have a perpetual reference.

We have also seen that the interest of the king and of the governing aristocracy is directly the reverse; it is to have unlimited power over the rest of the community, and to use it for their own advantage. In the supposed case of the balance of the monarchical, aristocratical, and democratical powers, it cannot be for the interest of either the monarchy or the aristocracy to combine with the democracy; because it is the interest of the democracy, or community at large, that neither the king nor the aristocracy should have one particle of power, or one particle of the wealth of the community, for their own advantage.

The democracy or community have all possible motives to

endeavor to prevent the monarchy and aristocracy from exercising power, or obtaining the wealth of the community, for their own advantage. The monarchy and aristocracy have all possible motives for endeavoring to obtain unlimited power over the persons and property of the community. The consequence is inevitable: they have all possible motives for combining to obtain that power, and unless the people have power enough to be a match for both, they have no protection. The balance, therefore, is a thing the existence of which, upon the best possible evidence, is to be regarded as impossible. The appearances which have given color to the supposition are altogether delusive.

VI

IN THE REPRESENTATIVE SYSTEM ALONE THE SECURITIES FOR GOOD GOVERNMENT ARE TO BE FOUND

WHAT, then, is to be done? For according to this reasoning we may be told that good government appears to be impossible. The people as a body cannot perform the business of government for themselves. If the powers of government are entrusted to one man or a few men, and a monarchy or governing aristocracy is formed, the results are fatal; and it appears that a combination of the simple forms is impossible.

Notwithstanding the truth of these propositions, it is not yet proved that good government is unattainable. For though the people, who cannot exercise the powers of government themselves, must entrust them to some one individual or set of individuals, and such individuals will infallibly have the strongest motives to make a bad use of them, it is possible that checks may be found sufficient to prevent them. The next subject of inquiry, then, is the doctrine of checks. It is sufficiently conformable to the established and fashionable opinions to say that upon the right constitution of checks all goodness of government depends. To this proposition we fully subscribe. Nothing, therefore, can exceed the importance of correct conclusions upon this subject. After the developments already made, it is hoped that the inquiry will be neither intricate nor unsatisfactory.

In the grand discovery of modern times, the system of representation, the solution of all the difficulties both speculative and practical will perhaps be found. If it cannot, we seem to be forced upon the extraordinary conclusion that good government is impossible. For as there is no individual or combination of individuals, except the community itself, who would not have an interest in bad government if entrusted with its powers, and as the community itself is incapable of exercising those powers and must entrust them to some individual or combination of individuals, the conclusion is obvious: the community itself must check those individuals, else they will follow their interest and produce bad government.

But how is it the community can check? The community can act only when assembled; and then it is incapable of acting. The community, however, can choose representatives, and the question is whether the representatives of the community can operate as a check.

VII

WHAT IS REQUIRED IN A REPRESENTATIVE BODY TO MAKE IT A SECURITY FOR GOOD GOVERNMENT?

WE may begin by laying down two propositions which appear to involve a great portion of the inquiry, and about which it is unlikely that there will be any dispute.

1. The checking body must have a degree of power sufficient for the business of checking.

2. It must have an identity of interest with the community, otherwise it will make a mischievous use of its power.

1. To measure the degree of power which is requisite upon any occasion, we must consider the degree of power which is necessary to be overcome. Just as much as suffices for that purpose is requisite, and no more. We have then to inquire what

power it is which the representatives of the community, acting as a check, need power to overcome. The answer here is easily given. It is all that power, wheresoever lodged, which they in whose hands it is lodged have an interest in misusing. We have already seen that to whomsoever the community entrusts the powers of government, whether one or a few, they have an interest in misusing them. All the power, therefore, which the one or the few, or which the one and the few combined, can apply to insure the accomplishment of their sinister ends, the checking body must have power to overcome otherwise its check will be unavailing. In other words, there will be no check.

This is so exceedingly evident that we hardly think it necessary to say another word in illustration of it. If a king is prompted by the inherent principles of human nature to seek the gratification of his will, and if he finds an obstacle in that pursuit, he removes it, of course, if he can. If any man or any set of men oppose him, he overcomes them if he is able; and to prevent him they must, at the least, have equal power with himself.

The same is the case with an aristocracy. To oppose them with success in pursuing their interest at the expense of the community, the checking body must have power successfully to resist whatever power they possess. If there is both a king and an aristocracy, and if they would combine to put down the checking force and to pursue their mutual interest at the expense of the community, the checking body must have sufficient power successfully to resist the united power of both king and aristocracy.

These conclusions are not only indisputable, but the very theory of the British constitution is erected upon them. The House of Commons, according to that theory, is the checking body. It is also an admitted doctrine that if the King had the power of bearing down any opposition to his will that could be made by the House of Commons, or if the King and the House of Lords combined had the power of bearing down its opposition to their joint will, it would cease to have the power of checking them; it must, therefore, have a power sufficient to overcome the united power of both.

2. All the questions which relate to the degree of power necessary to be given to that checking body, on the perfection of whose operations all the goodness of government depends, are thus pretty easily solved. The grand difficulty consists in finding the means of constituting a checking body the power of which shall not be turned against the community for whose protection it is created.

There can be no doubt that if power is granted to a body of men, called representatives, they, like any other men, will use their power, not for the advantage of the community, but for their own advantage, if they can. The only question is, therefore, how they can be prevented; in other words, how are the interests of the representatives to be identified with those of the community?

Each representative may be considered in two capacities: in his capacity of representative, in which he has the exercise of power over others, and in his capacity of member of the community, in which others have the exercise of power over him.

If things were so arranged that, in his capacity of representative, it would be impossible for him to do himself so much good by misgovernment as he would do himself harm in his capacity of member of the community, the object would be accomplished. We have already seen that the amount of power assigned to the checking body cannot be diminished beyond a certain amount. It must be sufficient to overcome all resistance on the part of all those in whose hands the powers of government are lodged. But if the power assigned to the representative cannot be diminished in amount, there is only one other way in which it can be diminished, and that is in duration.

This, then, is the instrument: lessening of duration is the instrument by which, if by anything, the object is to be attained. The smaller the period of time during which any man retains his capacity of representative, as compared with the time in which he is simply a member of the community, the more difficult it will be to compensate the sacrifice of the interests of the longer period by the profits of misgovernment during the shorter.

This is an old and approved method of identifying as nearly as possible the interests of those who rule with the interests of those who are ruled. It is in pursuance of this advantage that the members of the British House of Commons have always been chosen for a limited period. If the members were hereditary, or even if they were chosen for life, every inquirer would immediately pronounce that they would employ, for their own advantage, the powers entrusted to them, and that they would go just as far in abusing the persons and properties of the people as their estimate of the powers and spirit of the people to resist them would allow them to contemplate as safe.

As it thus appears, by the consent of all men, from the time when the Romans made their consuls annual down to the present day, that the end is to be attained by limiting the duration either of the acting or (which is better) of the checking power, the next question is, to what degree should the limitation proceed?

The general answer is plain. It should proceed till met by overbalancing inconveniences on the other side. What, then, are the inconveniences which are likely to flow from a too-limited duration?

They are of two sorts: those which affect the performance of the service for which the individuals are chosen, and those which arise from the trouble of election. It is sufficiently obvious that the business of government requires time to perform it. The matter must be proposed and deliberated upon; a resolution must be taken and executed. If the powers of government were to be shifted from one set of hands to another every day, the business of government could not proceed. Two conclusions, then, we may adopt with perfect certainty: that whatsoever time is necessary to perform the periodical round of the stated operations of government should be allotted to those who are invested with the checking powers; and, secondly, that no time which is not necessary for that purpose should by any means be allotted to them. With respect to the inconvenience arising from frequency of election, though it is evident that the trouble of election, which is always something, should not be repeated oftener than is necessary, no great allowance will need to be made for it, because it may easily be reduced to an inconsiderable amount.

As it thus appears that limiting the duration of their power is a security against the sinister interest of the people's representatives, so it appears that it is the only security of which the nature of the case admits. The only other means which could be employed to that end would be punishment on account of abuse. It is easy, however, to see that punishment could not be effectually applied. Previous to punishment, definition is required of the punishable acts, and proof must be established of the commission. But abuses of power may be carried to a great extent without allowing the means of proving a determinate offense. No part of political experience is more perfect than this.

If the limiting of duration be the only security, it is unnecessary to speak of the importance which ought to be attached to it.

In the principle of limiting the duration of the power delegated to the representatives of the people is not included the idea of changing them. The same individual may be chosen any number of times. The check of the short period for which he is chosen, and during which he can promote his sinister interest, is the same upon the man who has been chosen and rechosen twenty times as upon the man who has been chosen for the first time. And there is good reason for always re-electing the man who has done his duty, because the longer he serves, the better acquainted he becomes with the business of the service. Upon this principle of rechoosing, or of the permanency of the individual, united with the power of change, has been recommended the plan of permanent service with perpetual power of removal. This, it has been said, re-

duces the period within which the representative can promote
his sinister interest to the narrowest possible limits; because
the moment when his constituents begin to suspect him, that
moment they may turn him out. On the other hand, if he con-
tinues faithful, the trouble of election is performed once for
all, and the man serves as long as he lives. Some disadvantages,
on the other hand, would accompany this plan. The present,
however, is not the occasion on which the balance of different plans is capable of being adjusted.

VIII

WHAT IS REQUIRED IN THE ELECTIVE BODY TO SECURE THE REQUISITE PROPERTIES IN THE REPRESENTATIVE BODY

HAVING considered the means which are capable of being employed for identifying the interest of the representatives, when
chosen, with that of the persons who choose them, it remains
that we endeavor to bring to view the principles which ought
to guide in determining who the persons are by whom the act
of choosing ought to be performed.

It is most evident that upon this question everything depends. It can be of no consequence to insure, by shortness of
duration, a conformity between the conduct of the representatives and the will of those who appoint them, if those who
appoint them have an interest opposite to that of the community, because those who choose will, according to the principles of human nature, make choice of such persons as will
act according to their wishes. As this is a direct inference from
the very principle on which government itself is founded, we
assume it as indisputable.

We have seen already that if one man has power over others
placed in his hands, he will make use of it for an evil purpose
—for the purpose of rendering those other men the abject
instruments of his will. If we, then, suppose that one man
has the power of choosing the representatives of the people, it
follows that he will choose men who will use their power as

representatives for the promotion of this his sinister interest.

We have likewise seen that, when a few men have power given them over others, they will make use of it exactly for the same ends and to the same extent as the one man. It equally follows that, if a small number of men have the choice of the representatives, such representatives will be chosen as will promote the interests of that small number by reducing, if possible, the rest of the community to be the abject and helpless slaves of their will.

In all these cases, it is obvious and indisputable that all the benefits of the representative system are lost. The representative system is, in that case, only an operose and clumsy machinery for doing that which might as well be done without it—reducing the community to subjection under the *one* or the *few.*

When we say the "few," it is seen that, in this case, it is of no importance whether we mean a few hundreds, or a few thousands, or even many thousands. The operation of the sinister interest is the same, and the fate is the same of all that part of the community over whom the power is exercised. A numerous aristocracy has never been found to be less oppressive than an aristocracy confined to a few.

The general conclusion, therefore, which is evidently established is this, that the benefits of the representative system are lost in all cases in which the interests of the choosing body are not the same with those of the community.

It is very evident that, if the community itself were the choosing body, the interest of the community and that of the choosing body would be the same. The question is whether that of any portion of the community, if erected into the choosing body, would remain the same?

One thing is pretty clear, that all those individuals whose interests are indisputably included in those of other individuals may be struck off without inconvenience. In this light may be viewed all children, up to a certain age, whose interests are involved in those of their parents. In this light, also, women may be regarded, the interest of almost all of whom is involved either in that of their fathers or in that of their husbands.

Having ascertained that an interest identical with that of the whole community is to be found in the aggregate males of an age to be regarded as *sui juris,* who may be regarded as the natural representatives of the whole population, we have to go on and inquire whether this requisite quality may not be found in some less number, some aliquot part of that body.

As degrees of mental qualities are not easily ascertained, outward and visible signs must be taken to distinguish, for this purpose, one part of these males from another. Applicable signs of this description appear to be three: years, property, profession or mode of life.

According to the first of these means of distinction, a portion of the males, to any degree limited, may be taken by prescribing an advanced period of life at which the power of voting for a representative should commence. According to the second, the elective body may be limited by allowing a vote to those only who possess a certain amount of property or of income. According to the third, it may be limited by allowing a vote only to such persons as belong to certain professions or certain connections and interests. What we have to inquire is, if the interest of the number, limited and set apart, upon any of those principles, as the organ of choice for a body of representatives, will be the same with the interest of the community?

With respect to the first principle of selection, that of age, it would appear that a considerable latitude may be taken without inconvenience. Suppose the age of forty were prescribed as that at which the right of suffrage should commence; scarcely any laws could be made for the benefit of all the men of forty which would not be laws for the benefit of all the rest of the community.

The great principle of security here is that the men of forty have a deep interest in the welfare of the younger men, for otherwise it might be objected, with perfect truth, that, if decisive power were placed in the hands of men of forty years of age, they would have an interest, just as any other detached portion of the community, in pursuing that career which we have already described—for reducing the rest of the community to the state of abject slaves. But the great majority of old men have sons, whose interest they regard as an essential part of their own. This is a law of human nature. There is, therefore, no great danger that, in such an arrangement as this, the interests of the young would be greatly sacrificed to those of the old.

We come next to the inquiry, whether the interest of a body of electors, constituted by the possession of a certain amount of property or income, would be the same with the interest of the community?

It will not be disputed that, if the qualification were raised so high that only a few hundreds possessed it, the case would be exactly the same with that of the consignment of the electoral suffrage to an aristocracy. This we have already considered and have seen that it differs in form rather than substance from a simple aristocracy. We have likewise seen that it alters not the case in regard to the community, whether the aristocracy be some hundreds or many thousands. One thing is, therefore, completely ascertained, that a pecuniary qualification, unless it were very low, would only create an aristocratical government and produce all the evils which we have shown to belong to that organ of misrule.

This question, however, deserves to be a little more minutely considered. Let us next take the opposite extreme. Let us suppose that the qualification is very low, so low as to include the great majority of the people. It would not be easy for the people who have very little property to separate their interests from those of the people who have none. It is not the interest of those who have little property to give undue advantages to the possession of property, which those who have the great portions of it would turn against themselves.

It may, therefore, be said that there would be no evil in a low qualification. It can hardly be said, however, on the other hand, that there would be any good, for if the whole mass of the people who have some property would make a good choice, it will hardly be pretended that, added to them, the comparatively small number of those who have none, and whose minds are naturally and almost necessarily governed by the minds of those who have, would be able to make the choice a bad one.

We have ascertained, therefore, two points. We have ascertained that a very low qualification is of no use, as affording no security for a good choice beyond that which would exist if no pecuniary qualification was required. We have likewise ascertained that a qualification so high as to constitute an aristocracy of wealth, though it were a very numerous one, would leave the community without protection and exposed to all the evils of unbridled power. The only question, therefore, is whether, between these extremes, there is any qualification which would remove the right of suffrage from the people of small or of no property, and yet constitute an elective body, the interest of which would be identical with that of the community?

It is not easy to find any satisfactory principle to guide us in our researches and to tell us where we should fix. The qualification must either be such as to embrace the majority of the population or something less than the majority. Suppose, in the first place, that it embraces the majority, the question is whether the majority would have an interest in oppressing those who, upon this supposition, would be deprived of political power? If we reduce the calculation to its elements, we shall see that the interest which they would have of this deplorable kind, though it would be something, would not be very great. Each man of the majority, if the majority were constituted the governing body, would have something less than the benefit of oppressing a single man. If the majority were twice as great as the minority, each man of the majority would only have one-half the benefit of oppressing a single man. In that case, the benefits of good government, accruing to all, might be expected to overbalance to the several members of such an elective body the benefits of misrule peculiar to themselves. Good government would, therefore, have a tolerable security. Suppose, in the second place, that the qualification did not admit a body of electors so large as the majority; in that case, taking again the calculation in its elements, we shall see that each man would have a benefit equal to that derived from the oppression of more than one man, and that, in proportion as the elective body constituted a smaller and smaller minority, the benefit of misrule to the elective body would be increased and bad government would be insured.

It seems hardly necessary to carry the analysis of the pecuniary qualification as the principle for choosing an elective body any further.

We have only remaining the third plan for constituting an elective body. According to the scheme in question, the best elective body is that which consists of certain classes, professions, or fraternities. The notion is that, when these fraternities or bodies are represented, the community itself is represented. The way in which, according to the patrons of this theory, the effect is brought about is this: Though it is perfectly true that each of these fraternities would profit by misrule and have the strongest interest in promoting it, yet, if three or four such fraternities are appointed to act in conjunction, they will not profit by misrule and will have an interest in nothing but good government.

This theory of representation we shall not attempt to trace further back than the year 1793. In the debate on the motion of Mr. (now Earl) Grey for a reform in the system of representation, on the 6th of May of that year, Mr. Jenkinson, the present Earl of Liverpool, brought forward this theory of representation, and urged it in opposition to all idea of reform in the British House of Commons, in terms as clear and distinct as those in which it has recently been clothed by leading men on both sides of that House. We shall transcribe the passage from the speech of Mr. Jenkinson, omitting, for the sake of abbreviation, all those expressions which are unnecessary for conveying a knowledge of the plan and of the reasons upon which it was founded:

Supposing it agreed (he said) that the House of Commons is meant to be a legislative body, representing all descriptions of men in the country, he supposed every person would agree that the landed interest ought to have the preponderant weight. The landed interest was, in fact, the *stamina* of the country. In the second place, in a commercial country like this, the manufacturing and commercial interest ought to have a considerable weight, secondary to the landed interest, but secondary to the landed interest only. But was this all that was necessary? There were other descriptions of people, which, to distinguish them from those already mentioned, he should style professional people, and whom he considered as absolutely necessary to the composition of a House of Commons. By "professional people" he meant those members of the House of Commons who wished to raise themselves to the great offices of the State; those that were in the army, those that were in the navy, those that were in the law.

He then, as a reason for desiring to have those whom he calls "professional people" in the composition of the House of Commons, gives it as a fact that country gentlemen and merchants seldom desire, and seldom have motives for desiring, to be ministers and other great officers of state. These ministers and officers, however, ought to be made out of the House of Commons. Therefore, you ought to have "professional people" of whom to make them. Nor was this all:

There was another reason why these persons were absolutely necessary. We were constantly in the habit of discussing in that House all the important concerns of the State. It was necessary, therefore, that there should be persons in the practice of debating such questions.

There was a third reason which, to his mind, was stronger than all the rest. Suppose that in that House there were only country gentlemen, they would not then be the representatives of the nation, but of the landholders. Suppose there were in that House only commercial persons, they would not be the representatives of the nation, but of the commercial interest of the nation. Suppose the landed and commercial interest could both find their way into the House, the landed interest would be able, if it had nothing but the commercial interest to combat with, to prevent that interest from having its due weight in the constitution. All descriptions of persons in the country would thus, in fact, be at the mercy of the land-holders.

He adds,

the professional persons are, then, what makes this House the representatives of the people. They have collectively no *esprit de corps,* and prevent any *esprit de corps* from affecting the proceedings of the House. Neither the landed nor commercial interest can materially affect each other, and the interests of the different professions of the country are fairly considered. The Honorable gentleman (Mr. Grey) and the petition on this table rather proposed uniformity of election. His ideas were the reverse—that the modes of election ought to be as varied as possible, because, if there was but one mode of election, there would, generally speaking, be but one description of persons in that House, and by a varied mode of election only could that variety be secured.

There is great vagueness undoubtedly in the language here employed, and abundant wavering and uncertainty in the ideas. But the ideas regarding this theory appear in the same half-formed state in every speech and writing in which we have seen it adduced. The mist, indeed, by which it has been kept surrounded alone creates the difficulty, because it cannot be known precisely how anything is good or bad till it is precisely known what it is.

According to the ideas of Lord Liverpool, the landholders ought to be represented; the merchants and manufacturers ought to be represented; the officers of the army and navy ought to be represented; and the practitioners of the law ought to be represented. Other patrons of the scheme have added that literary men ought to be represented. And these, we believe, are almost all the fraternities which have been named for this purpose by any of the advocates of representation by clubs. To insure the choice of representatives of the landholders, landholders must be the choosers; to insure the choice of representatives of the merchants and manufacturers, merchants and manufacturers must be the choosers; and so with respect to the other fraternities, whether few or many. Thus it must be at least in *substance*, whatever the form under which the visible acts may be performed. According to the scheme in question, these several fraternities are represented *directly*, the rest of the community is *not* represented directly, but it will be said by the patrons of the scheme that it is represented *virtually*, which, in this case, answers the same purpose.

From what has already been ascertained, it will appear certain that each of these fraternities has its sinister interest and will be led to seek the benefit of misrule if it is able to obtain it. This is frankly and distinctly avowed by Lord Liverpool. And by those by whom it is not avowed, it seems impossible to suppose that it should be disputed.

Let us now, then, observe the very principle upon which this theory must be supported. Three or four or five or more clubs of men have unlimited power over the whole community put into their hands. These clubs have, each and all of them, an interest, an interest the same with that which governs all other rulers in misgovernment—in converting the persons and properties of the rest of the community wholly to their own benefit. Having this interest, says the theory, they will not make use of it but will use all their powers for the benefit of the community. Unless this proposition can be supported, the theory is one of the shallowest **by** which the pretenders to political wisdom have ever exposed themselves.

Let us resume the proposition. Three or four or five fraternities of men, composing a small part of the community, have all the powers of government placed in their hands. If they oppose and contend with one another, they will be unable to convert these powers to their own benefit. If they agree, they will be able to convert them wholly to their own benefit and to do with the rest of the community just what they please. The patrons of this system of representation assume that these fraternities will be sure to take that course which is *contrary* to their interest. The course which is *according* to their interest appears as if it had never presented itself to their imaginations!

There being two courses which the clubs may pursue, one contrary to their interest, the other agreeable to it, the patrons of the club system must prove, they must place it beyond all doubt, that the clubs will follow the first course, and not follow the second; if not, the world will laugh at a theory which is founded upon a direct contradiction of one of the fundamental principles of human nature.

In supposing that clubs or societies of men are governed, like men individually, by their interests, we are surely following a pretty complete experience. In the idea that a certain number of those clubs can unite to pursue a common interest, there is surely nothing more extraordinary than that as many individuals should unite to pursue a common interest. Lord Liverpool talks of an *esprit de corps* belonging to a class of landholders made up of the different bodies of landholders in every county in the kingdom. He talks of an *esprit de corps* in a class of merchants and manufacturers made up of the different bodies of merchants and manufacturers in the several great towns and manufacturing districts in the kingdom. What, then, is meant by an *esprit de corps?* Nothing else but a union for the pursuit of a common interest. To the several clubs supposed in the present theory, a common interest is created by the very circumstance of their composing the representing and represented bodies. Unless the patrons of this theory can prove to us, contrary to all experience, that a common interest cannot create an *esprit de corps* in men in combinations as well as in men individually, we are under the necessity of believing that an *esprit de corps* would be formed in the classes separated from the rest of the community for the purposes of representation; that they would pursue their common interest and inflict all the evils upon the rest of the community to which the pursuit of that interest would lead.

It is not included in the idea of this union for the pursuit of a common interest that the clubs or sets of persons appropriated to the business of representation should totally harmonize. There would, no doubt, be a great mixture of agreement and disagreement among them. But there would, if experience is any guide, or if the general laws of human nature have any power, be sufficient agreement to prevent their losing sight of the common interest; in other words, for insuring all that abuse of power which is useful to the parties by whom it is exercised.

The real effect of this motley representation, therefore, would only be to create a motley aristocracy, and, of course, to insure that kind of misgovernment which it is the nature of aristocracy to produce, and to produce equally whether it is a uniform or a variegated aristocracy, whether an aristocracy all of landowners, or an aristocracy in part landowners, in part merchants and manufacturers, in part officers of the army and navy, and in part lawyers.

We have now, therefore, examined the principles of the representative system and have found in it all that is necessary to constitute a security for good government. We have seen in what manner it is possible to prevent in the representatives the rise of an interest different from that of the parties who choose them—namely, by giving them little time, not dependent upon the will of those parties. We have likewise seen in what manner identity of interest may be insured between the electoral body and the rest of the community. We have, therefore, discovered the means by which identity of interest may be insured between the representatives and the community at large. We have, by consequence, obtained an organ of government which possesses that quality without which there can be no good government.

IX

1. OBJECTION: THAT A PERFECT REPRESENTATIVE SYSTEM, IF ESTABLISHED, WOULD DESTROY THE MONARCHY AND THE HOUSE OF LORDS

THE question remains whether this organ is competent to the performance of the whole of the business of government? And it may be certainly answered that it is not. It may be competent to the making of laws, and it may watch over their execution; but to the executive functions themselves, operations in detail, to be performed by individuals, it is manifestly not competent. The executive functions of government consist of two parts, the administrative and the judicial. The administrative, in this country, belong to the king; and it will appear indubitable that, if the best mode of disposing of the administrative powers of government be to place them in the hands of one great functionary, not elective but hereditary, a king such as ours, instead of being inconsistent with the representative system in its highest state of perfection, would be an indispensable branch of a good government; and, even if it did not previously exist, would be established by a representative body whose interests were identified, as above, with those of the nation.

The same reasoning will apply exactly to our House of Lords. Suppose it true that, for the perfect performance of the business of legislation and of watching over the execution of the laws, a second deliberative assembly is necessary, and that an assembly such as the British House of Lords, composed of the proprietors of the greatest landed estates, with dignities and privileges, is the best adapted to the end: it follows that a body of representatives, whose interests were identified with those of the nation, would establish such an assembly if it did not previously exist, for the best of all possible reasons—that they would have motives for, and none at all against it.

Those parties, therefore, who reason against any measures necessary for identifying the interests of the representative body with those of the nation, under the plea that such a representative body would abolish the King and the House of Lords, are wholly inconsistent with themselves. They maintain that a King and a House of Lords, such as ours, are important and necessary branches of a good government. It is demonstratively certain that a representative body, the interests of which were identified with those of the nation, would have no motive to abolish them if they were not causes of bad government. Those persons, therefore, who affirm that, it would certainly abolish them affirm implicitly that they are causes of bad, and not necessary to good government. This oversight of theirs is truly surprising.

The whole of this chain of reasoning is dependent, as we stated at the beginning, upon the principle that the acts of men will be conformable to their interests. Upon this principle we conceive that the chain is complete and irrefragable. The principle, also, appears to stand upon a strong foundation. It is indisputable that the acts of men follow their will, that their will follows their desires, and that their desires are generated by their apprehensions of good or evil; in other words, by their interests.

X

2. OBJECTION: THAT THE PEOPLE ARE NOT CAPABLE OF ACTING AGREEABLY TO THEIR INTERESTS

THE apprehensions of the people respecting good and evil may be just, or they may be erroneous. If just, their actions will be agreeable to their real interests. If erroneous, they will not be agreeable to their real interests, but to a false supposition of interest.

We have seen that, unless the representative body are chosen by a portion of the community the interest of which cannot be made to differ from that of the community, the interest of the community will infallibly be sacrificed to the interest of the rulers.

The whole of that party of reasoners who support aristocratical power affirm that a portion of the community, the interest of whom cannot be made to differ from that of the community, will not act according to their interest, but contrary to their interest. All their pleas are grounded upon this assumption. Because if a portion of the community whose interest is the same with that of the community would act agreeably to their own interest, they would act agreeably to the interest of the community, and the end of government would be obtained.

If this assumption of theirs is true, the prospect of mankind is deplorable. To the evils of misgovernment they are subject by inexorable destiny. If the powers of government are placed in the hands of persons whose interests are not identified with those of the community, the interests of the community are wholly sacrificed to those of the rulers. If so much as a checking power is held by the community, or by any part of the community where the interests are the same as those of the community, the holders of that checking power will not, according to the assumption in question, make use of it in a way agreeable, but in a way contrary, to their own interest. According to this theory, the choice is placed between the evils which will be produced by design—the design of those who have the power of oppressing the rest of the community, and an interest in doing it—and the evils which may be produced by mistake—the mistake of those who, if they acted agreeably to their own interest, would act well.

Supposing that this theory were true, it would still be a question between these two sets of evils: whether the evils arising from the design of those who have motives to employ the powers of government for the purpose of reducing the community to the state of abject slaves of their will or the evils arising from the misconduct of those who never produce evil but when they mistake their own interest are the greatest evils.

Upon the most general and summary view of this question it appears that the proper answer cannot be doubtful. They who have a fixed, invariable interest in acting ill, will act ill invariably. They who act ill from mistake will often act well, sometimes even by accident, and in every case in which they are enabled to understand their interest, by design.

There is another and a still more important ground of preference. The evils which are the produce of interest and power united, the evils on the one side, are altogether incurable: the effects are certain while that conjunction which is the cause of them remains. The evils which arise from mistake are not incurable; for if the parties who act contrary to their interest had a proper knowledge of that interest, they would act well. What is necessary, then, is knowledge. Knowledge on the part of those whose interests are the same as those of the community would be an adequate remedy. But knowledge is a thing which is capable of being increased; and the more it is increased, the more the evils on this side of the case would be reduced.

Supposing, then, the theory of will opposed to interest to be correct: the practical conclusion would be—as there is something of a remedy to the evils arising from this source, none whatever to the evils arising from the conjunction of power and sinister interest—to adopt the side which has the remedy, and to do whatever is necessary for obtaining the remedy in its greatest possible strength, and for applying it with the greatest possible efficacy.

It is no longer deniable that a high degree of knowledge is capable of being conveyed to such a portion of the community as would have interests the same with those of the community. This being the only resource for good government, those who say that it is not yet attained stand in this dilemma: either they do not desire good government, which is the case with all those who derive advantage from bad, or they will be seen employing their utmost exertions to increase the quantity of knowledge in the body of the community.

The practical conclusion, then, is actually the same, whether we embrace or reject the assumption that the community are little capable of acting according to their own interest. That assumption, however, deserves to be considered. And it would need a more minute consideration than the space to which we are confined will enable us to bestow upon it.

One caution, first of all, we should take along with us, and it is this: that all those persons who hold the powers of government without having an identity of interests with the community, all those persons who share in the profits which are made by the abuse of those powers, and all those persons whom the example and representations of the two first classes influence, will be sure to represent the community, or a part having an identity of interest with the community, as incapable in the highest degree of acting according to their own interest; it being clear that they who have not an identity of interest with the community ought to hold the powers of government no longer if those who have that identity of interest could be expected to act in any tolerable conformity with their interest. All representations from that quarter, therefore, of their incapability so to act are to be received with suspicion. They come from interested parties; they come from parties who have the strongest possible interest to deceive themselves, and to endeavor to deceive others. It is impossible that the interested endeavors of all those parties should not propagate, and for a long time successfully uphold, such an opinion—to whatever degree it might be found upon accurate inquiry to be without foundation.

A parallel case may be given. It was the interest of the priesthood, when the people of Europe were all of one religion, that the laity should take their opinions exclusively from them, because in that case the laity might be rendered subservient to the will of the clergy to any possible extent; and as all opinions were to be derived professedly from the Bible, they withdrew from the laity the privilege of reading it. When the opinions which produced the Reformation, and all the blessings which may be traced to it, began to ferment, the privilege of the Bible was demanded. The demand was resisted by the clergy upon the very same assumption which we have now under contemplation. "The people did not understand their own interest. They would be sure to make a bad use of the Bible. They would derive from it not right opinions, but all sorts of wrong opinions." [1]

There can be no doubt that the assumption in the religious case was borne out by still stronger appearance of evidence

[1] A most instructive display of these and similar artifices for the preservation of mischievous power, after the spirit of the times is felt to be hostile to it, may be seen in Father Paul's *History of the Council of Trent.*

than it is in the political. The majority of the people may be supposed less capable of deriving correct opinions from the Bible than of judging who is the best man to act as a representative.

Experience has fully displayed the nature of the assumption in regard to religion. The power bestowed upon the people of judging for themselves has been productive of good effects, to a degree which has totally altered the condition of human nature and exalted man to what may be called a different stage of existence. For what reason, then, is it we are called upon to believe that if a portion of the community having an identity of interests with the whole community have the power of choosing representatives, they will act wholly contrary to their interests and make a bad choice?

Experience, it will be said, establishes this conclusion. We see that the people do not act according to their interests, but very often in opposition to them.

The question is between a portion of the community which if entrusted with power would have an interest in making a bad use of it and a portion which, though entrusted with power, would not have an interest in making a bad use of it. The former are any small number whatsoever who, by the circumstance of being entrusted with power, are constituted an aristocracy.

From the frequency, however great, with which those who compose the mass of the community act in opposition to their interests, no conclusion can in this case be drawn without a comparison of the frequency with which those who are placed in contrast with them act in opposition to theirs. Now it may with great confidence be affirmed that as great a proportion of those who compose the aristocratical body of any country as of those who compose the rest of the community are distinguished for a conduct unfavorable to their interests. Prudence is a more general characteristic of the people who are without the advantages of fortune than of the people who have been thoroughly subject to their corruptive operation. It may surely be said that if the powers of government must be entrusted to persons incapable of good conduct, they were better entrusted to incapables who have an interest in good government than to incapables who have an interest in bad.

It will be said that a conclusion ought not to be drawn from the unthinking conduct of the great majority of an aristocratical body against the capability of such a body for acting wisely in the management of public affairs, because the body will always contain a certain proportion of wise men, and the rest will be governed by them. Nothing but this can be said with pertinency. And under certain modifications this may be said with truth. The wise and good in any class of men do, to all general purposes, govern the rest. The comparison, however, must go on. Of that body whose interests are identified with those of the community it may also be said that, if one portion of them are unthinking there is another portion wise; and that, in matters of state, the less wise would be governed by the more wise, not less certainly than in that body whose interests, if they were entrusted with power, could not be identified with those of the community.

If we compare in each of these two contrasted bodies the two descriptions of persons, we shall not find that the foolish part of the democratical body are more foolish than that of the aristocratical, nor the wise part less wise. Though according to the opinions which fashion has propagated it may appear a little paradoxical, we shall probably find the very reverse.

That there is not only as great a proportion of wise men in that part of the community which is not the aristocracy as in that which is, but that under the present state of education and the diffusion of knowledge there is a much greater, we presume there are few persons who will be disposed to dispute. It is to be observed that the class which is universally described as both the most wise and the most virtuous part of the community, the middle rank, are wholly included in that part of the community which is not the aristocratical. It is also not disputed that in Great Britain the middle rank are numerous and form a large proportion of the whole body of the people. Another proposition may be stated, with a perfect confidence of the concurrence of all those men who have attentively considered the formation of opinions in the great body of society, or, indeed, the principles of human nature in general. It is, that the opinions of that class of the people who are below the middle rank are formed, and their minds are directed by that intelligent, that virtuous rank who come the most immediately in contact with them, who are in the constant habit of intimate communication with them, to whom they fly for advice and assistance in all their numerous difficulties, upon whom they feel an immediate and daily dependence in health and in sickness, in infancy and in old age; to whom their children look up as models for their imitation, whose opinions they hear daily repeated and account it their honor to adopt. There can be no doubt that the middle rank, which gives to science, to art, and to legislation itself their most distinguished ornaments, and is the chief source of all that has exalted and refined human nature, is that portion of the community of which, if the basis of representation were ever so far extended, the opinion would ultimately decide. Of the people beneath them a vast majority would be sure to be guided by their advice and example.

The incidents which have been urged as exceptions to this general rule, and even as reasons for rejecting it, may be considered as contributing to its proof. What signify the irregularities of a mob, more than half composed, in the greater number of instances, of boys and women, and disturbing for a few hours or days a particular town? What signifies the occasional turbulence of a manufacturing district, peculiarly unhappy from a very great deficiency of a middle rank, as there the population almost wholly consists of rich manufacturers and poor workmen—with whose minds no pains are taken by anybody, with whose afflictions there is no virtuous family of the middle rank to sympathize, whose children have no good example of such a family to see and to admire, and who are placed in the highly unfavorable situation of fluctuating between very high wages in one year and very low wages in another? It is altogether futile with regard to the foundation of good government to say that this or the other portion of the people may at this or the other time depart from the wisdom of the middle rank. It is enough that the great majority of the people never cease to be guided by that rank; and we may, with some confidence, challenge the adversaries of the people to produce a single instance to the contrary in the history of the world.

(F. F.)

The Library of Liberal Arts

LEIBNIZ, G., Monadology and Other Philosophical Essays

LESSING, G., Laocoön

LOCKE, J., A Letter Concerning Toleration
Second Treatise of Government

LONGINUS, On Great Writing (On the Sublime)

LUCIAN, Selected Works

LUCRETIUS, On Nature

MACHIAVELLI, N., The Art of War
Mandragola

MARCUS AURELIUS, Meditations

MEAD, G., Selected Writings

MILL, J., An Essay on Government

MILL, J. S., Autobiography
Considerations on Representative Government
Nature *and* Utility of Religion
On Liberty
On the Logic of the Moral Sciences
Theism
Utilitarianism

MOLIÈRE, Tartuffe

MONTESQUIEU, C., The Persian Letters

NIETZSCHE, F., The Use and Abuse of History

NOVALIS, Hymns to the Night and Other Writings

OCKHAM, W., Philosophical Writings

PAINE, T., The Age of Reason

PALEY, W., Natural Theology

PARKINSON, T., ed., Masterworks of Prose

PICO DELLA MIRANDOLA, On the Dignity of Man, On Being and the One, *and* Heptaplus

PLATO, Epistles
Euthydemus
Euthyphro, Apology, Crito
Gorgias
Meno
Phaedo
Phaedrus
Protagoras
Statesman
Symposium
Theaetetus
Timaeus

Commentaries:
BLUCK, R., Plato's Phaedo
CORNFORD, F., Plato and Parmenides
Plato's Cosmology
Plato's Theory of Knowledge
HACKFORTH, R., Plato's Examination of Pleasure
Plato's Phaedo
Plato's Phaedrus

PLAUTUS, The Haunted House
The Menaechmi
The Rope

POPE, A., An Essay on Man

POST, C., ed., Significant Cases in British Constitutional Law

QUINTILIAN, On the Early Education of the Citizen-Orator

REYNOLDS, J., Discourses on Art

Roman Drama, Copley and Hadas, trans.

ROSENMEYER, OSTWALD, and HALPORN, The Meters of Greek and Latin Poetry

RUSSELL, B., Philosophy of Science

Sappho, The Poems of

SCHILLER, J., Wilhelm Tell

SCHLEGEL, J., On Imitation and
    Other Essays

SCHNEIDER, H., Sources of
    Contemporary
    Philosophical Realism
    in America

SCHOPENHAUER, A., On the Basis
    of Morality
    Freedom of the Will

SELBY-BIGGE, L., British Moralists

SENECA, Medea
    Oedipus
    Thyestes

SHAFTESBURY, A., Characteristics

SHELLEY, P., A Defence of Poetry

SMITH, A., The Wealth of Nations
    (Selections)

Song of Roland, Terry, trans.

SOPHOCLES, Electra

SPIEGELBERG, H., The Socratic
    Enigma

SPINOZA, B., Earlier Philosophical
    Writings
    On the Improvement of the
    Understanding

TERENCE, The Brothers
    The Eunuch
    The Mother-in-Law
    Phormio
    The Self-Tormentor
    The Woman of Andros

Three Greek Romances, Hadas,
    trans.

TOLSTOY, L., What is Art?

VERGIL, Aeneid

VICO, G. B., On the Study Methods
    Our Time

VOLTAIRE, Philosophical Letters

WHITEHEAD, A., Interpretation of
    Science

WOLFF, C., Preliminary Discourse
    on Philosophy in General

XENOPHON, Recollections of
    Socrates *and* Socrates'
    Defense Before the Jury